A Contested
EUROPE

A Contested EUROPE

Polemics, Papers and Essays

GYÖRGY SCHÖPFLIN

H P

H P

KKL Publications LLC, Helena History Press
Reno, Nevada USA
Publishing scholarship about and from Central and East Europe
www.helenahistorypress.com

Distributed by IngramSpark and available through all major e-retail sites
info@helenahistorypress.com

ISBN: 978-1-943596-09-6

Copy Editor: Krisztina Kós

Table of Contents

Preface by Zsolt Németh vii

Foreword by Katalin Kádár Lynn ix

Thanks ix

Introduction 1

History and the Historians 21

After 1945: Cold War, Cold Peace 43

Central Europe: Kundera, Incompleteness, Lack of Agency 49

Liberalism, Human Rights, Populism 67

Political lessons for Central Europe from Orbán's Hungary 79

Hungary: the Fidesz Project 93

An Epistemological Crisis 103

Orbán, Illiberalism 121

Swings and Roundabouts? The Growing Gap between
Western and Central Europe 127

Interview (transcription) with Sofia Metelkina 143

What If? 159

Hungary after the First World War 167

EU Law and Politics: the Rule of Law Framework 185

Nationhood, Modernity, Democracy:
Manifestations of National Identity in Modern Europe 191

Preface

There were few—if any—Hungarians among our contemporaries who could write about Europe and the European Union with the same intellectual depth and credibility as György Schöpflin did. Prior to his death in 2021, György Schöpflin was—as a practicing politician—Member of the European Parliament representing a Hungarian political party, Fidesz-KDNP, for 15 years.

Previously, as a descendant of a renowned emigrant family, he studied in Britain, where he lived and worked in exile. He taught at British universities for many years, was a researcher at Chatham House, but also worked for the BBC before embarking on a political career. From the beginning of the regime change in 1989–90, he consciously chose the intellectual community of Fidesz as his political family, built close friendship with the founders and intellectuals of the party. He actively attended the very first and then numerous subsequent Bálványos Summer Free Universities in Romania. György Schöpflin gave intellectual weight and authority to the Hungarian center-right political community having deep Hungarian national commitment.

As an extremely productive author he has published books, written a series of essays and articles both during his years in the United Kingdom and later, too. As an esteemed and sought-after speaker at international conferences, he primarily sought answers to the problems of national minorities, national identity, nationalism and Central and Eastern European politics. His works, his speeches in the European Parliament and his conference presentations were characterized by an eclectic style coupled with superior professional knowledge, which always contained the subtle, delicate and, unfortunately, vanishing English irony.

The volume is the work of a par excellence européer. Today, we can confidently say that this is the will of György Schöpflin, which reflects the rather contradictory changes in the European Union in recent years, but is also accompanied by the author's fear: "The disintegration of the Union would be a disaster for Hungary" and the whole continent!

This hope does not prevent him from revealing with surgical precision the disruptions of the spirituality and institutional functioning of the European Union, or explaining in great detail that he believes: the European Union is heading in the wrong direction today. The volume should be a "must-read" from university students on the subject to practicing politicians for anyone who participates responsibly in the affairs of their political community like members of the demos of ancient city-states!

Zsolt Németh,
MP, Chairman of Committee on Foreign Affairs, Hungary

Foreword

We at Helena History Press are deeply honored to release the English edition of George Schopflin's *A Contested Europe,* the last major work emanating from the pen of one of the most distinguished political scientists dealing with matters related to Central and East Europe in the 20th Century. This English edition was in galleys when he passed away in November of 2021.

We mourn his passing and offer this volume as a tribute to the author, to his years of dedication to scholarship, his generous support of emerging scholars and for his gentlemanly yet rigorous analysis of contemporary affairs within Europe and the world. His service in European Parliament as a Hungarian delegate for FIDESZ from 2004–2019 provided him with a unique perspective on the European Union and its myriad challenges. Always an independent thinker, György Schöpflin did not need to take a back seat to anyone intellectually. Prior to serving in European Parliament, he had a distinguished academic career that culminated as Jean Monnet Professor of Politics at the School of Slavonic and East European Studies, University of London.

We were pleased to work with him translating and bringing the memoir of General Vilmos Nagybaczoni Nagy to the reading public for which he wrote the Introduction. Professor Schöpflin knew of the memoir and its historically valuable observations and asked us to publish the book, a first-person account by a key participant in the decision making of the Hungarian government during WWII.

It was our great privilege to work with György Schöflin in the last decade of his life. His legacy includes this, his last important work which showcases the range and depth of his analysis of the European Union and its member states. A must read for scholars of modern Europe.

Reno Nevada 4/21/22

Katalin Kádár Lynn PhD
Editor in Chief/ Publisher
Helena History Press LLC

Thanks

It is customary to offer a long list of those who have helped the author in completing the text, always with the rider that faults, flaws and fallacies are the author's own. So be it, done. I would like to thank the editors of *Hungarian Review* for publishing my articles and above all to my loyal parliamentary team Emese Csörsz, Dóra Czifra and Gertrúd Kendernay-Nagyidai for their company, suggestions and infinite patience. And for taking care of me. It's been a pleasure working with you.

Introduction

I have called this section "Introduction", but it might be more accurate to use either prolegomena or Allgeimeines Teil. What I'm trying to convey here is that these preliminary comments apply as methodological and structural principles to the entirety of the text, and can be seen as guides to interpretation.

This collection of articles were written over several years, in that sense they were occasional pieces, but as the occasion was generally much the same, they have a certain intellectual coherence. Readers should note that I closed the text with the end of June 2019 to coincide with the end of my time as a member of the European Parliament. As a *terminus ad quem*, it's no more arbitrary than any other.

What has been happening in Europe, why has there been friction between the European Union and Central Europe, notably Hungary? What has Fidesz been trying to achieve? Why is nationhood still around, contrary to liberal expectations? What has happened to Central Europe after the end of communism?

In this book, I have put together a thoughtful synthesis, drawing on my thoroughly unusual, even unorthodox intellectual hinterland. Near enough uniquely, I write as someone with a deep background in political theory and political practice. I taught at the University of London for the best part of three decades and then spent a decade and a half as a Hungarian member of the European Parliament.

These papers and polemics reflect this twofold background. They are controversial in challenging established perspectives, going against the mainstream on issues like nationhood and liberalism. At the same time, the argument is based on a deep knowledge of Europe as itself and Europe of the European Union – they are not the same – and, not surprisingly, a thoroughgoing understanding of Central Europe, not just Hungary, obviously, but the other countries and nations of the region. It is in this positive sense that the book is multicultural, it builds its argument on the broad Central European past and present.

I have a few thoughts on the methodology that underlies this text. The motto of the London School of Economics is *rerum cognoscere causas*, to learn the causes of things or, in more elevated language, to understand the aetiology, notably that correlation is not causation. This means looking at structures and processes and taking note of necessary and sufficient conditions. The accumulation of data is often interesting and the construction of a narrative based on this data can be useful, but useful or not, writing a narrative requires the selection of one's data and then we, the readers, would like to know the selection criteria. This is where the social sciences at their best – I should stress that "best" – do something different from history, and why the turf war between the two has no ending. Causation is, freely admitted, difficult to isolate when human actors are concerned. This is the realm of the double hermeneutic and of relational sociology which seek to understand human action and its causes in interactivity.

Second, I believe very firmly in the message of the Enlightenment, that there is no privileged knowledge, that any and all questions can be asked, even when there is a strong taboo in play. And these are frequent enough. This introduction is written in the era of "trigger warnings", "safe spaces", "privilege", "no platforming" as delegitimating rhetorical devices, accusations of racism (ditto) – these are all sacralised propositions, hedged in with taboos and proclaimed apodictic. I see no reason why they should not be ignored or questioned or deconstructed. Indeed – how fashions change – two decades ago it was de rigueur to be transgressive and decentering. Does anyone still remember?

Third, and this should be an obligatory requirement, a duty even, that one's sources should be checked and data that do not confirm one's argument cannot be screened out. Furthermore, being clear about one's sources is fair to the reader. I know that some think this is showing off, others that so doing is blinding the reader with science, or, as was once thrown at me, disguising dubious propositions in scientific language, or yet others that reference to sources gets in the way of the argument. Not for me, it doesn't.

Fourth and last, the underlying and in places explicit issue is power – the uses of power, the asymmetries of power, agency, the reproduction of power, its legitimation and delegitimation. All of these demand some explication. Power will exist in all human relations and transactions. The neutrality of power is only to be found where there are no interactions and/or in the cemetery. Hence some regulation of power will always be established, whether this is brute force or a complex institutional framework like a code of law.

Human collectivities seek to ensure predictability, hence the codification. Enlightenment rationality came with a promise that once the mumbo-jumbo of religion was done away with, power would become rational and injustice would disappear. Codswallop. On the one hand, new sacred spaces and objects were constructed, on the other, Enlightenment rationality could not reconcile the asymmetries of power deriving from wealth or influence or birth or intelligence or knowledge or the incommensurability of values. Hence human institutions were and are always plagued by asymmetries and this has given rise to a current of ideas that suspects all power (except one's own, I rather imagine).

My own attitude to European integration should be clarified for the sake of fairness. I spent a postgraduate year at the College of Europe (1962–1963) and what I learned there strengthened a predisposition to be generally in favour of a more closely integrated Europe. I don't think that I would have put it in these terms at the time, but the trauma of the war and as someone who lived through the siege of Budapest would have made me strongly committed to a never again attitude.

When elected to the European Parliament in 2004, I had lived in the UK for decades and had absorbed various British values (some Scots, some English), but I remained well disposed towards integration, especially after the slow, but irreversible emergence of an English national current that indubitably gained some of its energies from self-differentiation from the Continent. English nationhood, whether ethnic or civic or a melange, was something I could never identify with, as I realised in 1996 when football fans started to appear with English flags (white background, red cross).

Hence the idea of being close to the EU and to European integration as an MEP certainly appealed to me, quite apart from being a Hungarian MEP with extensive experience of the EU. But then, things changed over the years.

In 2005, France and the Netherlands rejected the Constitutional Treaty and that led me to the conclusion that a broad, strategic deepening did not have democratic support. And that placed a significant question mark over the integration project as a whole as far as I was concerned, given that the EU was simultaneously singing its commitment to democracy. I recall the then Portuguese prime minister, José Socrates saying in 2007 that democracy was Europe's DNA (chapeau to his speech writer). But then, how was integration to be reconciled with a democratic no?

Matters were made worse for me when I started encountering the European federalists. Listening to them as I did, I was forced to conclude that they had something in common with other single issue visionaries – they would brook no counter-argument, thereby abandoning one of Europe's central values, reasoned argument. I have a particular memory of an address by the great German sociologist Ulrich Beck in 2010 (I think), whose triumphalism reminded me of the way in which nationalists used rhetorics, obviously the content having been different. It was thoroughly off-putting for me and I gradually understood that there was no place for me in the Europe that Beck and his confrères were advocating.

After 2010, when Fidesz came to power and I was no longer an opposition MEP, matters became worse, as an entirely irrational wave of hostility to Fidesz swept through the pro-Europeans (discussed elsewhere in this book). None of this hostility was evidence-based, thereby again there was an abandonment of European values by the left. Worse, integration was increasingly appropriated by the left, parallel to the monopoly ownership claim over democracy by what called itself liberalism. Indeed, what we have today is a hegemonic claim by liberalism that there is only one Europe – theirs. All else was anti-European, Europhobic, Eurosceptic, quite apart from the scattering of words like populism, nativism, xenophobia, illiberalism, racism, fascism, Nazism etc. What this slow turn in attitudes created was the denial of any possibility of reform of integration that was not sanctioned by the monopoly. And there I parted company.

So I became Eurocritical, a category not recognised by the Manicheans of the left. I continue to see integration as strategically desirable, but do not accept further integration as the answer to everything. There are, indeed, areas where a European level solution works best, like food safety, but this goes hand-in-hand with deep and irresoluble problems of democracy at the EU level.

I would argue that the complex relationship between the EU institutions – Commission, Parliament, Council, Court, agencies and agency-like bodies, high level working groups and, no doubt other bodies that operate outwith the glare of publicity – and the member states does add up to a European polis. But with the best will in the world, this polis does not meet the criteria of democracy. It is too remote from the citizens who are for all practical purposes unable to make inputs into policy making at the European level and are dismissed as populists if they try. I could at this point offer a lengthy account of the European Citizens' Initiative (see article 11 of the Treaty) seeing that I was Parliament's rapporteur on this file, but I'll exercise self-limitation in order to avoid drowning in technicalities. Suffice it to say, that the European polis does not welcome inputs from below unless they conform to the liberal integrationism of the elites.

The problem of the polis goes beyond remoteness. It is important to recognise that the two-level identification expected of citizens – being a citizen of Europe and a citizen of one's member state (the latter is necessary condition of the former, Article 9) – is a hard act to bring off. The identification is made yet more difficult by the deliberate weakening of the symbolic and ritualistic aspects of the European identity, these being essential parts of identity maintenance. Europe Day is celebrated, but its European dimension is weak, and the European flag has not really made a breakthrough into wider consciousness. In this light, the polis evidently does not have much of a demos. And can there be a democracy without a demos? The latter is a necessary condition of the former.

What is beyond dispute is that an enormous amount of power has accumulated in the polis, in the symbolic Brussels. And that's where further problems arise. Often enough this power is desirable and effective, like food safety or water pollution regulation, but – this where emergent properties are relevant – this power is greater than the sum of its parts and, for that matter, continues to accumulate. When I arrived in 2004, the *acquis communautaire*, the rule book, was around 120,000 pages (or so it was widely supposed). Currently, 15 years on, it's probably double that. This accumulation necessarily raises three issues that are central to democracy – accountability, transparency and feedback. On all three, the polis performs badly.

As far as accountability is concerned, Parliament's oversight is adequate on financial and budgetary matters, but decidedly less so when it comes to governance. By way of example, EU agencies are set up without much input from the wider public, there is a little from Parliament and there the matter ends. Lobbies, NGOs will play a role here, but their accountability does not exist. The media play no role in this process. Yet some agencies have the power to issue regulations and some, like Frontex or Galileo, have sizeable budgets and affect the citizens. In this area power is exercised technocratically, not least because what the power is used for is indeed highly technical. But that still leaves the strategic and governance side of things well beyond civic oversight.

Transparency looks better, at first sight anyway. In reality, and this is a central problem of state power everywhere, giving rise to the deep state issue or Nordlinger's autonomy of the state over society – there are decision-making processes that are informal and secretive. To be fair, transparency is an infinite demand and whatever is out in the open will be paralleled by processes in the background, with the result that what becomes public policy is de facto irreversible, because too many decisions have been taken informally and these then become the assumption set on the basis of which other policy is formulated. As far as Parliament is concerned, the plenary sessions are theatre and ritual, little else. Minds are not changed by these debates, they merely sanction decisions taken in committee. Occasionally, of course, a text adopted by committee is amended by plenary, for better or for worse, but these usually reflect party political interests and not the putative interest of the citizens, mythical or otherwise.

Feedback I've already touched on. There is some. Commissioners do visit the member states, MEPs do consult with their constituents, albeit it is very hard to communicate with one's voters whose understanding of the EU is overwhelmingly about the conflict between the member state and Brussels, because that is how the local media serve it up. From the point of view of the rulers of the polis, the Brussels elite, feedback is seldom welcome, because that can contradict the elite's way of doing things. Thus the campaigns against TTIP and glyphosate were not seen in Brussels as, oh how wonderful, the citizens are taking us seriously, far from it.

It is worth adding another shift here, one concerning the use of language. In the 2000s, there was widespread discussion of the EU's democratic deficit in EU circles. By 2019, that phrase had disappeared from common parlance. Shifts of this kind have their significance and my assessment of it is that it is linked causally with the undercurrent of popular discontent with the EU, with the consequent strengthening of its defences by the liberal elite which had quietly begun to monopolise its control over integration and, hence, was not really interested in popular inputs into the polis, other than at a formulaic level.

This did not, of course, mean that the deficit had disappeared or been countered; it was a cognitive screening out of a disagreeable factor that disturbed the liberal narrative of Europe. Thereby the definition of democracy itself was changed. The consent of the governed was downgraded and a vaguely defined "pluralism" had tacitly taken the place of consent. I recall an exchange with Frans Timmermans, the commissioner having charge of the EU institutional order, when he expressly defined democracy as being "pluralism". I insisted that democracy, to be worthy of the name, had to be based on the consent of governed. And, the killer thrust, added that China was indubitably pluralistic, but by no stretch of the imagination was it democratic.

One further aspect of the European polis requires attention here, the role of legality and the courts. One of the lessons I learned while visiting Canada (as a member of a parliamentary delegation) was that legality on its own is not enough, there must also be legitimacy. This is a lesson that the European polis stolidly ignores, not surprisingly as it has little time for the demos. The ultimate authority of the European polis is the Treaty which raises two pivotal questions. One is Treaty amendment, which means amending Kelsen's *Grundnorm*, the basis of the system, and the other is the interpretation of the Treaty. Amending the Treaty is slow and difficult because it means ratification in all the member states. Whatever happens in the polis, it needs a legal base and that base is the Treaty, it's the ultimate authority in all EU matters. But the Treaty and its interpretation mean looking at those responsible for so doing.

One of the features of contemporary politics, not just in the EU, is the role of the judiciary in determining political issues. This is a controversial area, because increasingly political problems are decided by the courts and arguably there is a legitimacy gap here. Judges are not elected, and I would not want them to be elected as that would thoroughly politicise the legal system, but the judiciary should recognise that its power should be exercised with due regard to self-limitation. Juristocracy raises two further points, one of them widely discussed, the other less so. How judges, especially constitutional court judges, are chosen is a political act, but only partly so. Judges are human beings and, hence, have political views, but that does not necessarily make them the handmaidens of party political power.

There is a widespread proposition that the Hungarian constitutional court has been packed by Fidesz cronies. This story is repeatedly spread by the opposition, but it does not stand up to closer scrutiny. First, constitutional court judges are appointed by parliament by a two-thirds majority, meaning that the Fidesz government, as indeed its predecessors, had to craft balanced deals for the election to succeed and did so even when it did have the necessary majority. Second, and this proposition is simply ignored, those appointed are legal professionals and that professionalism regularly overrides politicisation. Thirdly, constitutional courts in the polis do operate within a European network and, therefore, cannot afford to lose the esteem of their peers. And if one looks at the practice of other EU states, then the question of "cronies" is never raised. When Laurent Fabius was appointed to the French Conseil Constitutionel, no one called him an Hollande crony. Et pourquoi non? Was Scalia a Reagan crony?

The other, much less visible area affecting juristocracy is the role of the apparatus, the administrative staff of the judges. Their influence in preparing judgements is enormous and wholly invisible. They generally have a deep knowledge of the case law at hand and are – according to those affected – ready to impose their ideas on the judges, making the latter not much more than mouthpieces for their staff. There have certainly been complaints in this area, notably from an anonymous judge of the European Court of Human Rights in Strasbourg. This makes oversight of judicial power even more difficult to practise than might appear at first sight.

Axiomatically, the demos has next to no input into what the legal system decides, hence judicial power – juristocracy – has become a something like a "wicked" problem, one for which there is no satisfactory solution. How far should judicial power stretch and can it be made accountable? Is it possible to avoid the legalisation of politics and, worse, the politicisation of the law? In the world of the EU, the European polis, the answer is increasingly no. This raises real dangers, as both political power and the independence of the law are discredited.

There are no easy answers and in the case of the European polis, the EUCJ, the Luxembourg Court, customarily takes decisions by pro-integrationist criteria. That in turn raises the question of the limits of European versus member state constitutionality and the growing emphasis by member state constitutional courts on the country's constitutional identity. Are the two on collision course? Can legality and legitimacy be reconciled in the European polis? We don't know, but this issue will certainly play a role in the functioning of the polis, for good or ill.

Juristocracy has a further dimension that is only seldom formulated in these terms, if at all. Membership of the EU is voluntary and one of the founding principles of integration was respect for the interests of all member states. Increasingly, but especially in the 2014–2019 parliament, there were growing demands from the left for the polis to acquire punitive instruments. The rule of law Framework of 2014 was one of these. Parliament's report on democracy, rule of law and fundamental rights was another. The process can be said to have culminated with the Sargentini report (2018), which entirely dispensed with the European values of debate and hearing the other side, *audi et alteram partem*. It was directly and incontrovertibly punitive. But can a European polis function at all if conflict resolution is replaced by punishment, the voluntary principle is disregarded and the view of the governed is dismissed as populism? Obviously my answer is no, because a polis of this kind would be moving or actually is moving towards a liberal authoritarianism.

There is another side to all this which I will call the Simmel-Coser effect. This really should be better known to public opinion – media, NGOs, politicians. In simple terms the authors of the effect, both classics of sociology, argue that putting pressure on a collectivity has unintended consequences, mostly a strengthening of the group's will to resist rather than to obey humbly. Indeed, conflict will increase the cohesion of the group, help to mobilise its energies and intensify the will to resist. Crucially (from Simmel), conflict is interpreted to mean that one's antagonist does not recognise one's collectivity as moral community, thereby coming close to rejecting one as members of humanity.

And once a reciprocal antagonism has been established, it is very difficult indeed to dismantle it – that demands an effort of will from both parties and a tacit recognition that they committed an error in launching the polarisation.

It will be clear from the argument in this book that the pressures on Poland and Hungary, the two primary targets of a punitive-minded EU, were not started by these states, but by the EU. There were faults on both sides, there invariably are, but the process of punishment then fed back into the EU to underpin its new identity as a site of power with the capacity to discipline its supposedly erring members. Brexit enhanced this, but note that the moves against Hungary and Poland began well before 2016. In both cases, the conflict showed up the weaknesses in the polis. If membership of the polis is voluntary, and Brexit demonstrates that it is (thanks to Article 50), then those targeted by the punitive left could reasonably conclude that something was amiss, that they were being required to conform to something to which they had not signed up. After all, one can argue about the interpretations of Article 2 of the Treaty, the one that supposedly codified "European values" – a weasel-like phrase if ever there was one – given that the Article mentions the rights of minorities, but whenever any of my colleagues tried to raise issues of malfeasance by ethnic majorities against ethnic minorities (as in Transylvania), Timmermans's office threw it back as nothing to do with them, because this was a matter of member state competence. Or so they had decided.

This illuminates another dimension of the punitive polis – consistency. There really is nothing like a double standard to discredit and delegitimate a power holder than being caught out in an inconsistency. If you come out and say it directly, we are punishing you because you are Hungarian, that is deplorable, but it is consistent. But if you are acting in the name of the polis and claiming to enforce a single, universal standard, as the EU does, and then apply the punitive procedure selectively, then you're in trouble. Your legitimacy is shot in the eyes of the target group, even if the punishers approve. I was very taken by what the Netherlands prime minister, Mark Rutte, said to parliament in 2018, quoting a Dutch saying (and, yes, I checked with a Dutch friend, it really does exist), "trust arrives on foot and leaves on horseback".

So if the polis is to become a discipline and punish entity, and there is every sign that it is moving in this direction at the time of writing (June 2019), in as much as there is strong pressure to set up a rule of law monitoring mechanism, then it had better make absolutely sure that it applies its rules with absolute even-handedness and equity, that it does everything that it humanly can to avoid the fatal embrace of taking seemingly legal decisions by political, above all, party political criteria. The Sargentini report was an obvious case of just that.

To illustrate the nature of the problem, I recall another exchange with Frans Timmermans, this time about constitutional courts and the Article 7 procedure launched by the Commission (not Parliament) against Poland. I pointed out that while there may well have been problems in Poland with the constitutional tribunal (court), there were analogous issues in Slovakia, in Spain, in Slovenia, in the Czech Republic and maybe elsewhere. He looked rather awkward at this data and replied that the Commission did not have the capacity to monitor these flaws in the constitutional order. I confess to having been flabbergasted. How could the EU claim that it was applying sanctions against one member state because it was supposedly in breach of Article 2 values and ignoring similar problems in other member states? Was there a single standard or not? Was the EU – the polis – a single legal space or not? If it was, then the procedure against Poland was weakly grounded as long as other states were allowed their dysfunctional constitutional courts. If the EU was not a single legal space, then it had no right to intervene in Poland at all. I fear this logic of mine ended up nowhere fast. It was dismissed as "whataboutism". This failure to understand the destructive effects of double standards will haunt the EU and could cause serious disruption in the polis.

Then, a few words about Brexit. Not the actual Brexit process, much of which I witnessed with a kind of horrified fascination at the sheer inability and/or unwillingness of the British political class to pay any attention to the EU as a political actor, as a polis protecting its interests, but what I'm going to call the Brexit effect. Here I want to go back to another of the classics of sociology, to Hirschman's *Exit, Voice and Loyalty*. The basic proposition is straightforward enough. If an actor is dissatisfied, he or she has three choices – giving up, exit; complaining, voice; or staying inside, loyalty. It should be noted here that Hirschman discusses expulsion as a variant of exit, but there is no provision for this in the EU, only voluntary exit (Article 50).

Brexit is evidently a case of exit. And exit was seen as a possible attractive option in the thinking of Eurosceptic and Europhobic parties. But then came the travails of Brexit, both the complexity of the negotiations, the asymmetry of power between the EU and the UK and the dawning of the costs of exit. This reality was a different kind of exit from the one envisaged by Hirschman, that a customer stops buying a product. Brexit is and will be highly disruptive in that once the UK becomes a third state, and one without any agreement with the EU, value chains will be broken, the highly efficient British services industry (banks, insurance, finance) will not have the right to operate in the EU, airlines will exit from the Single Sky agreement and much else. I have the sense that while it was possible to conceptualise these costs theoretically, it was not until the process became visible in real terms that other potentials exiteers began to reassess their positions.

This has now happened, after all, everyone has had three years to look at the mess. But the outcome was not entirely predictable. Eurosceptic parties basically shifted their approach and became Eurocritical to a greater or lesser extent. What I mean by this is that they recognised the values of the polis, like the single market or Schengen, and concluded that they were better off reforming the EU from within. This was a logical move, an unintended consequence of action, and it dismayed the liberal elite. This is understandable. It is easy enough to fend off those who want to leave or dismantle an institution. Institutions have great resilience and defensive capabilities. But it is much more difficult to cope with internal opponents, who claim loyalty, but seek to change the terms on which that loyalty is predicated.

The success of the Eurocriticals in the 2019 parliamentary elections was not as great as they had expected, there was no breakthrough, but these forces are certainly strong enough to make the functioning of the 2019–2024 parliament different enough from its predecessors. The integrationists will have a much more difficult task ahead of them, the make-up of the polis has shifted. The dividing lines are clearly there in the European Parliament, they certainly exist in Council and in the member states, but they are rather less significant in the Commission which is heavily federalist. So, amending Hirschman's language, the polis will have to contend with no further exit, with a louder voice and disloyalty.

Historically, that is to say in the 1950s, one of the roles of integration was not only to ensure peace, but to transfer the lessons of democracy to the supra-state level. Central among these lessons is dealing with asymmetries of power. Such asymmetries are particularly acute in Europe where historically multiple sites of power were able to maintain themselves and were repeatedly engaged in conflict. The 20th-century catastrophes brought with them the realisation that there were better ways of conflict resolution than warfare (*pace* Clausewitz). So conflict resolution was one of the key objectives of integration. In many ways, this worked. As is argued elsewhere in this collection, conflict resolution is no longer as central to the integration process as it was. The Commission, the guardian of the Treaties, seems less concerned with this than previously.

This is particularly striking in the context of globalisation. Globalisation has brought into being new sites of power, inside and outside Europe, whereby new, previously unknown asymmetries are impacting on the polis. One example – the Chinese cultural revolution of the 1960s – did not affect Europe in any palpable way, but if China were to be caught up in some analogous turmoil now, Europe and the rest of the world would feel the backwash.

Two of these new – in reality old, but previously marginal – sources of asymmetry are worth exploring. They are relevant to what follows. The first of these is the asymmetry of centre-periphery relations. One can start out from Wallerstein's formulation, but currently it is clear enough that peripheries are no longer merely international, but have become a feature of the state level. In other words, peripheries, marked by less power, weaker agency, inaudible voice, have become a feature of the polis generally and its institutions particularly. Christophe Guilluy's formulation of peripheries in France can be readily applied to the EU as such and to the member states, as in the growing gap between capital cities and the rest of the country. But parallel asymmetries can be seen sociologically as between the mobile, knowledge based Anywheres of David Goodhart's analysis, as against the much less mobile sectors of society, his Somewheres, those more rooted in space and time.

The European polis pays next to no attention, other than occasional nods towards developing a social Europe. Yet this asymmetry is driving Eurocritical attitudes, the ones translated into political power through the European Parliamentary elections and the defence of intergovernmentalism by the member states (some of them, anyway). This is not a Central European deviancy. The resistance of the Hansa states of northern Europe to fiscal profligacy is structurally similar to the complaints of Central Europeans discussed later. And it is worth recalling the "54 conditions" of the Netherland's government from 2013, that there should be no further deepening or integration in 54 areas. A particular piquancy of this declaration is that it was introduced by the then Dutch foreign minister, Frans Timmermans, yes, the same Timmermans who as Commission's first vice-president became one of the prime agents of ever greater deepening. Well, we can't be consistent all of the time.

The other area of asymmetry is the one that can be identified through complexity theory. Complexity is driven by globalisation and the EU's problem is that in many ways, it remains a pre-globalisation institution. It continues to work on the assumption that emergent properties play no role, that accumulation of power in Brussels has only those consequences that are clear and visible. Then, a second flawed assumption is that the relationship between cause and effect is proportional. This is true of some situations, but all too often the butterfly effect creates havoc, via unintended consequences, ones ignored by the actors of the polis.

Third, linear processes, as in water invariably boiling at 100°C, are accompanied and confused by non-linearity, as in sectors of public opinion rejecting the linear assumptions of ever closer union, especially when this means rejecting what voters want and imposing a "European" solution on a member state, like parachuting in a Euro-conform prime minister into the Italian government. Then, there are positive feedback loops which intensify stresses in the system and make it impossible to return to equilibrium state, to stability in other words. Change begets more change and the centre can no longer control the periphery. Outcomes are uncertain and initiatives generate resistance. The dream of the Monnet method of integration, that each and every integrative step is uniformly implemented throughout the polis, is just that, a dream. It is unsustainable, because some processes are irreversible and move towards chaos.

A final, rather speculative problem concerns what the polis is, how it can be characterised. Obviously, it is not a state nor a country nor a republic nor a monarchy nor is it a commonwealth; it is neither a federation nor a confederation, though it may have some of the features of all of them. There is another possibility, namely that the European polis is beginning to resemble a liberal empire and, indeed, some approve because that would sideline the demos problem, not least because the demos is too open to the attractions of nationhood. Empires need some acquiescence in their rule, but the active support of the governed that democracy presupposes is superfluous. Those who favour the empire argument do so because empires marginalise nations and, therefore, nationalism. And national mobilisation continues to be seen as the primary obstacle to further expansion or deepening of the liberal empire concept. All the same, it is difficult to see how the polis-as-empire can be reconciled with any variant of democracy.

There is another dimension to this empire issue, one that cannot be proved, but the connection is suggestive and ties in with the 2015 migrant crisis. All the states of the West had overseas empires at one time or another, even while Austria and Russia had landward empires – Germany had both. The insight offered here is that the imperial legacy lives on, long after the empire itself has disappeared, albeit in a different form. There is what might be called an imperial thought-style that, in brief, believes that the country in question has a role that goes beyond its existing frontiers. This can also be negative, in the sense of post-colonial guilt, the near obsessive insistence that the West is guilty and there will always be something for which one can and should feel guilty (Bruckner). This thought-style manifests itself in language like "having a seat at the top table" or "punching above one's weight" and finds articulation in positive attitudes towards globalisation. The negative polarity of the phenomenon is the constant apologising for the colonial past and the sense that Europe owes the rest of the world. Movements like "Rhodes must fall", the campaign to have Cecil Rhodes's statue removed from an Oxford college is another manifestation of the same and ties in with the fervent need to rewrite history.

In an indirect fashion, the mobile Anywheres of Goodhart's analysis are the indirect descendants (or, who knows, the direct descendants) of the colonial officials who went out "to rule the natives" or uphold the *mission civilisatrice* (in the French case). I always thought it wonderfully surrealistic that in French Africa, children were taught that the Gauls were their ancestors; I'm not sure that Astérix would have approved or that the Africans would have enjoyed the sanglier rôti that the Gauls would feast on, but I digress.

More to the point is that this post-imperial thought-style, guilt and all, impelled Western elites to accept inward migration from non-Europe as a moral obligation and, this is crucial, sought to impose this moral obligation on the rest of Europe, Central Europe very much included. The Central Europeans, on the other hand, being former colonies and semicolonies – a status never accepted by the West – refused to accept the guilt and the obligation.

In 2017, Lubomír Zaorálek, then Czech foreign minister, made this more or less explicit (Wintour). The West had a terrible record, he noted, and had to confront the resentments of those whom they had colonised, but Central Europe was exempt from this and by implication had no reason to share the West's guilt, from which it followed, that Central

Europe had no particular reason to take in extra-European immigrants, but could take them or leave them. This argument did not go down with the West at all well, hence it was ignored mostly or rejected as arrogance. Looked at from a somewhat different angle, Hirschman's voice got nowhere. The subaltern can always speak, of course, but that does not mean that anyone will actually hear the message. The falconer has stopped listening to the falcon.

This does, however, imply that political power and legal provision are pointing in different directions. Legally, there is no hierarchy in the polis. The Treaty is crystal clear on this, viz. Article 4:

> The Union shall respect the equality of Member States before the Treaties as well as their national identities, inherent in their fundamental structures, political and constitutional, inclusive of regional and local self-government. It shall respect their essential State functions, including ensuring the territorial integrity of the State, maintaining law and order and safeguarding national security.

And by the same token, the Treaty explicitly declares that the competences of the EU are exclusively those that have actually been conferred on the EU by the member states. Here is Article 5:

> The limits of Union competences are governed by the principle of conferral. The use of Union competences is governed by the principles of subsidiarity and proportionality.

The political practice of the polis ignores this. The examples mentioned in the foregoing – the Framework, the Sargentini report – manifestly contradict the "equality of Member States".

So there is a contradiction. It illustrates nicely the argument made in the foregoing that the construction of an empire within the framework of the European polis is in no way alien to liberal integrationism. Indeed, there is a nice fit between the imperial thought-style and the polis-as-empire. Empire builders see themselves as acting in the name of a higher good. Historically this was divine right. The liberal imperialists of the European polis seem to be acting in the belief that they are guided by history. Belief is the right word here, the pressure to attain the further integration of the polis is centrally driven by faith and takes no note of factors that point in a different direction.

And if that means ignoring or evading the provisions of Treaty or disregarding the voters or sidelining counter-arguments – too bad.

References

Bruckner, Pascal. *The Tyranny of Guilt*. Translated by Steve Rendall. Princeton: Princeton University Press, 2010.

Coser, Lewis A. *The Functions of Social Conflict*. New York: Free Press, 1956.

Goodhart, David. *The Road to Somewhere: The Populist Revolt and the Future of Politics*. London: Hurst, 2017.

Guilluy, Christophe. *No Society: La fin de la classe moyenne occidentale*. Paris: Flammarion, 2018.

Hirschman, Albert O. *Exit, Voice, and Loyalty: responses to Decline in Firms, Organizations and States*. Cambridge MA: Harvard University Press, 1970.

Netherlands Government. "European where necessary, national where possible", News item | 21-06-2013 | 15:36. https://www.government.nl/latest/news/2013/06/21/european-where-necessary-national-where-possible. 2013. Accessed 22 June 2019.

Simmel, Georg. *Conflict and the Web of Group Affiliations*. New York: Free Press, 1955.

Urry, John. *Global Complexity*. London: Polity, 2003.

Wallerstein, Immanuel. *European Universalism: The Rhetoric of Power*. New York: The New Press, 2006.

Wintour, Patrick. "Growing awareness of colonial past fuels radicalisation, says Czech minister", *The Guardian*, 15 June 2017. https://www.theguardian.com/world/2017/jun/15/growing-awareness-of-colonial-past-fuels-radicalisation-says-czech-minister. Accessed 21 June 2019.

History and the Historians[*]

Multa novit vulpes, verum echinus unum magnum
(The fox knows many things, the hedgehog knows one big thing.
ARCHILOCUS, POPULARISED BY ISAIAH BERLIN.)

I have used the fox v. hedgehog metaphor to underscore one of the fundamental distinctions in the pursuit of knowledge.

The moving finger may have written and, yes, any amount of piety and wit may have been dispensed, yet that which has happened cannot be undone. Or so Fitzgerald's Khayyam would have us believe. I believed this too as a hedgehog. Now, in my vulpine identity, I see that the past is subject to constant reinterpretations, that history – the version of the past that we believe to be history – is hopelessly fluid and, ultimately, subjective.

That fluidity deters no one. The problem is I suspect a broader one. The world, certainly in its European manifestation, evidently believes that there is one history, a single history, which is objective, definitive, attainable and may or may not have a message (the last depends on whom you listen to). Furthermore, a historical fact is just that, a fact, usually, when deployed in this form, an incontrovertible fact. A secondary, but nonetheless important aspect of this is the assertion that the historian is, by his and her training, uniquely fitted to establish the facts, the truth, the light and possibly to decide what the message is. If there is one. So, for me, historians are hopelessly hedgehog fixated or just hedgehogs born.

[*] Originally published as "History and the Historians – Parts of a Memoir" in *Hungarian Review* X, no. 4 (2014), http://www.hungarianreview.com/article/20140514_history_and_the_historians_parts_of_a_memoir

To reach this one history, the crock of gold at the end of the rainbow, the historian must be equipped to perform certain tasks. Firstly, there is selection by non-explicit criteria. Second is linearity. The kind of history I am talking about is firmly chronological or, at any rate, following the temptation of a single logic. Then, third, is boundedness. History is about a limited set of events, from which extraneous elements have been shed (see firstly). Fourth, though less stringently, history is national, or at any rate, evidently coloured by the tacit assumptions, the doxa, of the historian, and these are far more national than historians will admit. Think of the very different traditions of history writing in French and in Anglo-Saxony.

Comparing the history of one country with another is not really *comme il faut*, because it turns into something not quite naturalised, maybe immanent is a better word, but in any case, illuminates the contingency of the (selected national) past, and thereby undermines any easy theory of causation. Indeed, contingency may well be the worst enemy that historians of the hedgehog kind have to contend with. Generally, they don't bother, they just screen it all out and assume somehow that because things happened in a particular order, they had to happen that way. This might well be called the TINA school of history. The proposition that by following this path the historian will certainly be importing an aetiology into her investigation of the past troubles her not at all. Post hoc, propter hoc? Just don't complicate matters, let alone use words like aetiology. After all, the task of the historian is to construct a historical narrative and not concern herself with the rest. Once we accept this, we can see that Hayden White was quite right, writing history is not qualitatively different from writing literature, though on hearing this the practitioners of both will certainly cry foul.

Yet some of them, the historians, may have an uneasy feeling that all is not well in the Temple of Clio and that their special space has been usurped by undesirables, like the foxes who smuggle multiple perspectives into their version of the past. The best of them anyway. There are, to be truthful, low grade foxes around who, having been captured by some erinacean thought pattern, like an ideology, will pretend to have vulpine qualities, but are in reality hedgehogs in disguise.

The Marxists, who follow the master and insist that history is the class struggle and will find class struggle in the whenever and wherever, are obvious candidates for pretend foxes. They may certainly illuminate some aspect of the past that conventional document crunching historians will have overlooked, but that is where their utility ends. Freudians, religious believers, localists, feminists, gender driven historians all have to struggle to escape the closure that their belief system imposes on them and often they do not succeed. I've had my encounters with several of them. I can recall meeting a woman at a conference who insisted that all history is a history of patriarchy and nothing else. It was a short conversation. After she pronounced this sentence, I discovered I had an urgent engagement in another part of the forest.

There is another danger in the world of document crunching, identified by James C. Scott in his *Zomia* book (p.34), to the effect that the density of evidence is in itself liable to lead historians astray. They find the rubble of the past and unconsciously assume that that's all the history there is. Quite apart from anything else, this approach to history tends to privilege the state, the ruler and elites. A cache of documents will distort perspective. Thereby they miss those people and phenomena whose texts, written, unwritten, are sparse or absent. Absence is difficult to chart, that something that should logically be there is not, but it can at times be remarkably illuminating.

The dead hand of positivism may well have moving fingers but whatever it does to set things down, what is written is only ever a partial account. Ok, say the readers, but how is one to write history without written evidence? Yes, well, that's where it's best to abandon positivism and to apply unorthodox (maybe that should be "unorthodox" from the historians' perspective) methods to assess the past.

The document obsession basically says that the archive is a sacred depository of the past, and the historian – so delighted by discovering documents, something concrete, written – cannot, will not see that a document is written primarily by one individual (or a team, making it more bland) with normal human characteristics, like being bad tempered or sleepy after a good lunch so that the information is contingent on other factors and is not "The Truth", quite apart from the fact that it will necessarily omit as much as it contains. The author of a dispatch will assume that his or her correspondent understands the emotional or intellectual context that has come into being between them and will allow meanings to be inferred. Can the archive-delving historian be sure that she really has grasped the context, that she can fully, objectively mirror the story? I greatly doubt it.

The alternative, to offer a collection of documents to the reader may be more honest, but again its objectivity is confounded by the devil of selection criteria. Why this document and not another? Well, because the historian is trying to make a case, to argue a thesis. An extreme case was of a doctoral dissertation on the international dimension of the Hungarian revolution of 1956. The student in question read documents in a variety of languages, including Russian and Hungarian (hats off), but did little more than to reproduce what she had read, expecting that this would prove her thesis, that the intervention by the Kremlin was not inevitable and could have been avoided by moderation on all sides. But she had no idea at all either of the significance of communist ideology as a factor affecting decision making in the Kremlin or of the intolerable tension in Hungary that resulted in a set of decisions that produced the invasion. Indeed, she firmly rejected that the events constituted a revolution and insisted that there was no difference, as far she was concerned, between a revolution, a revolt and an uprising. I should have asked her if, therefore, she would happily refer to the great French uprising of 1789 or the Russian revolt of 1917. I didn't, because although weak, the thesis was just about Ph.D. level and I didn't want to be faced with a rewritten version that would not, in my judgement, have been an improvement.

Then, there are the anecdotalists so much beloved of reviewers, who fight shy of complexity and theory, and generally pour scorn on technicality. They are two of a kind really, the anecdotalists and their reviewers, giving each other succour in an ever more complex world, who will readily assert that a good story will tell you more about some particular process or situation or transaction than any amount of analysis. This is nonsense of course. All that an anecdote tells you is a single instance that you extend to a collective phenomenon at your peril. But the insistence on the telling of a story and the preference for writing attractively do strengthen the Hayden White argument that, when push comes to shove, history is just a branch of literature. The hard reality is that if history is about more than the account of a single individual, in which case it is more akin to psychology than anything else, then it has to deal with collective phenomena. These may be a country, a nation, region, a city, a regiment, a trade union, a university or what you will, but they will by definition be about a collective experience.

And once we are in that part of the territory, the social sciences come into play. Concept formation, counterfactual conditionals, rational choice, free will, the notion of following a rule, the relation of sociology to psychology, intentions versus motives, reasons versus causes, values versus facts, qualitative versus quantitative change, statistical generalizations versus covering laws, theories of change, collective representations, identity theory, theories of power, relations between centre and periphery, elective affinities (as distinct from cause and effect), family relationships of institutions – to name only a few – all become necessary to understanding the past, even as they do to the present (quoting the TLS, 28 September 2012). The intuitive methods of the historians, attractive though they may be to the weaker brethren and sisters, will not produce anything more than literature, sometimes attractive, sometimes not. Much the same as the novel, really. No wonder that historians are deeply suspicious of and, indeed, positively hostile to the pervasive gaze of literary theory and semiotics. Once history writing is subjected to the disciplines of narratology, of genre theory, the claims to some kind of a supra-temporal, nay Platonic, objectivity begin to look distinctly threadbare.

There is a good deal to the argument that historians are the captives of linearity. They see that B follows A, and sort of assume, therefore, that there is (must be?) a causal relationship between them (or not as the case may be). They don't necessarily say this explicitly. But placing the two in conjunction allows the innocent reader to infer causation. Those who take aetiology seriously – is this a necessary condition of foxhood? – wince at this point. The answer to my rhetorical question is probably no, my guess is that foxes can be pretty carefree or, indeed, careless about causation. That archfox, Feyerabend, certainly indicated as much in his *Against Method* that I read many years ago, without necessarily understanding all of it. Still. I would like to believe that those who have moved on from linearity are also prepared to engage seriously with what is certainly the greatest problem in the social sciences.

Those who see no reason to think about causation, who vaguely assume that things happen because they happen and the task of the historian is to write about them elegantly (this has been described as the A.J.P. Taylor school of history writing) can easily fall into the trap of historical inevitability, even without being a Marxist, by the way. Other axiologies can do the same and have the same outcome, like a belief in "progress". The basic assumption is that what happened was the sole option, that counterfactual history is a fraud on the public which should be protected from such counterfeits and that alternatives, chance, accident, bad decision making are irrelevant. To my knowledge it was only Marxists of the hardest line Soviet kind who ever actually preached that history was law-governed. *Zakonomerny* was one of the few words of Russian that I have picked up over the years (I like the elegance of the Hungarian *törvényszerű*, even if I reject the concept unreservedly). But others, many of them at last count, fall all too easily into the same trap without even being aware of there being a trap at all. They assume that what happened was the sole pattern and will have nothing to do with the alternatives, the might-have-beens. This means that when assessing a decision, they tend to read history backwards and impute a message, a meaning, not to mention a clarity to the past that it does not have as lived present.

This wilful ignoring of human realities results in the historian's own human reality becoming the determinant, without this ever being acknowledged. When did you last read a historian who freely admitted that she might be mistaken?

All this can, and often does, bring into play a dogmatic defence of turf. Well, historians are, after all, human and have their prestige, status and even emoluments to protect. What I find a recurring event is the strong tendency on the part rather too many historians to take a sideswipe at the social sciences. My old friend, sadly the late Norman Stone, who writes a good prose style, found it necessary to state:

"Max Weber said that a new subject altogether needed to be invented, and he came up with *Politikwissenschaft*, political science. In due course, history had its revenge: political science utterly failed to do what any science should do, predict. In this case, predicting the fall of Communism. Right to the end, the political scientists, or Sovietologists, simply did not see what was happening under their noses."

This is not exactly true, some social scientists did, Zbigniew Brzezinski for one did so in his *Grand Failure*. Besides, prediction is not what the social sciences are there to do. To my mind, what they do at their best is to offer insights into collective human action, but applying the methodologies of the social sciences to the past is deeply disturbing to historians. Doing so challenges their monopoly and, worse, sometimes offers a more cogent view of human motivations in the past than the historians can manage with *their* methodologies. The bottom line as far as I am concerned is the double hermeneutic and reciprocal potentiation. I have written extensively about these and will not go over the same ground, but if a historian really can't get her head round the proposition that she too is subject to the ever-present contingency of the world, that she too has baggage, that she too comes to the topic with assumptions of her past, then there is nothing more to be said. Let her write and let what she has written be enjoyed (or not) as literature, but hardly as scientific objectivity.

Where does journalism end and history begin? There is a general proposition made by journalists that what they do best is to produce the first, rough draft of history. This is no more than an assertion, an untested one at that, indeed, a highly dubious one, because if we examine it closely – subject it to proper interrogation – then it generally turns out to be dubious if not actually mistaken. Why should journalists be able to seize the complexity of a situation and reflect it to their readers? What are their qualifications for this highly onerous task? What do journalists do with their personal baggage (or lack of it), with the immediate context, the dust, the chaos of war or civil strife, their lack of knowledge of the language? Ignore them, is the answer. Relying on interpreters is more risky than appears, they don't always translate accurately, have their own fears and desires, and the journalist has no means of double checking, if the thought occurs to her at all. The time pressure really doesn't help, it forces the journalist to file something now, at once, without further reflection, besides the story will be dead tomorrow – there is no day of reckoning, no answering to a higher instance.

Here too there are national divergences, self-evident to anyone who reads the press in more than one language. Anglo-Saxon journalists are, for the most part, trained in their craft to be straightforward, even simplistic, on the assumption that this is what their readers are capable of consuming. Over time, this becomes a self-fulfilling prophecy and readers stop expecting the media to reflect the complexity of a situation. On top of that, in the last 20 years media workers have been instructed (or so I assume) to be punchy and to be personal. The old ban on editorialising in reports has gone. Take what passes for an interview for example. The interviewee is no longer allowed to express his or her views at length, as the argument often demands, but these are reduced to the bits that the journalist thinks interesting. Does this not produce a distortion of the interviewee's views? Certainly, but who cares? So much for the first draft of history.

There is more, however. The standard average journalist will generally be unaware of his/her selection criteria – why point up this topic more than another. The criteria are deeply buried, and are at best intuitive, sometimes good, sometimes not. Of course, an experienced writer who has been allowed to acquire the necessary background in the area will be superior in translating the difference, but even he/she will be restricted by the sense that the audience will very likely be thoroughly ignorant of the topic covered. Think of the coverage of the Arab spring, for one. Formulae are a standard device to simplify things for the reader or viewer. The outcome can be rubbish. Two examples. During the Lebanese civil war in the 1970s and 1980s, the BBC invariably described the Christians as "right-wing" and the Druze as "Muslim". Really? Were all the Christians right-wing, every mother's son of them? In truth, the sheer complexity of Lebanon was enough to defeat most, if not all Western readers and viewers. "Muslim Druze"? It's about as accurate as talking about the "Buddhist Muslims".

Then during the Wars of Jugoslav Succession, BBC tv news would regularly show a shot of an artillery piece being fired. At whom, by whom, why, in what context? Oh no, don't tax the poor dears who are watching. During the Croatian military push into the Krajina and Bosnia, I found the BBC version of events impossible to make sense of, but as it happened, I came across a clear, concise explanation in the Austrian paper, Der Standard. When I mentioned this to a senior BBC wallah, he refused to listen and mumbled something about being fully satisfied by the BBC's coverage, which says more about the BBC's corporate culture and its understanding of the Corporation's proud motto, "nations shall speak truth unto nations" than anything else. Yes, the truth, but not if it's too difficult. The distinction between truth and reality passed them by completely.

Another much used technique is to begin a story with a person. It's a cliché and a major one, the old flawed belief that you can generalise from a single instance. The response of a single individual to a complex situation tells you only what that person thought, felt, wanted his interlocutor to believe on that particular day and nothing else. But that does not deter the journalists from using the technique that, presumably, they were taught at journalism school. So all this first draft stuff is just that, stuff with more than a dollop of nonsense to be added to the mix.

This still leaves open the question of what might be termed higher journalism, the melange of reportage, reflection, impressionistic writing, travelogues and the like. My sense of it is that as long as these are written as strictly first-person singular narratives, not claiming legitimacy by objectivity, they are perfectly enjoyable on their own terms and might even offer useful insights. The best yardstick for assessing the utility of this genre, a sub-genre of history to be sure, is to read their predecessors from 50 or 100 years ago. The prejudices of the authors will become evident at once, as will the dated perspective. A genuinely good example of the kind is Rebecca West's *Black Lamb and Grey Falcon*, a two-volume account of Jugoslavia written in the late 1930s. The pro-Serb bias of the author becomes obvious pretty quickly and she tended to exoticise the natives. That said, it's vivid, well written and thoughtful in places. But history? Objective? Hardly. I'm persuaded that the same will be said of other such works, say the clutch of books being produced about the Arab spring.

The rather rhetorical question I want to put it at this point, a *num* question, for those who remember their Latin, is it possible to write about the past without a theory of power, without understanding something about change and the mainsprings of collective action? Those who eschew this would do best to recognise that they are short-changing the reader and are offering, if not false coin, at least nothing more than an intuitive, personal account of events. And that account is only as good as the author's talent, just like the novelist's.

This takes us nicely to history as autobiography, an account inherently limited to and by one's experience and perceptions, a first-person narrative, but is more honest. First person singular descriptions can be vivid and truthful, but will always necessarily be a partial record, so to take the example of Ryszard Kapuściński: he may well have invented elements of his data – to lend verisimilitude to an otherwise bald and unconvincing narrative – but had he not said so and not pretended that he was producing the first, rough draft of history, his record would not now be in question. But because he is pigeonholed as a journalist, his narrative is rejected. Yet his writing reads beautifully, accept it as a part of literature, as (possibly) a consciously hybrid genre, which exists anyway, as "faction" or "fictionalised fact". It's just a matter of labelling, at the end of the day.

The Kapuściński story raises yet another issue, one that affects the social sciences too. How important, how significant are the personality and, above all, the political views of the historian? If the person in question held views that are currently despised, does that mean that her writing must also be transferred surreptitiously or with great ceremony to the scrapheap of history? Heidegger is most obviously the test case. Is his philosophy inherently "bad", maybe "Bad", because he joined the Nazis? There are many who would support this position as self-evident. It is a moral and emotional argument, though, not a rational one.

By the same token, should we reject Kapuściński because he maintained a fairly active relationship with the Polish secret services? Does this mean that his books are less readable, less vivid? My answer is certainly in the negative. But we can take this argument further, into the reductio ad absurdum category. By the common consent of his contemporaries, Tolstoy was a tiresome fellow; does that mean the we should regard his novels as equally tiresome? Hardly. Proust was awkward and could be disagreeable, Thomas Mann was stiff and maybe just a bit eccentric sexually. Same question, same answer, no?

So where should we draw the line between text and personality? Is it possible for a someone to be a morally reprehensible person and yet be the creator of major works of art? My answer is a resounding yes, but if not actually alone, I know that I am in a minority, that the current criteria of evaluation insist on conjoining the artist as a person and the artist as creator. The trouble with that approach is that it imports non-artistic criteria into the world of aesthetics, is reductionist and ultimately impoverishes the human experience. But, then, that's where hedgehogs can end up, all too easily, in the grip of moral (or some other kind of) monism.

In the 1980s, a time when I was beginning to study nations, nationalism and nationhood seriously, a considerable splash was made by Eric Hobsbawm (and his co-editor Terence Ranger) by publishing *The Invention of Tradition*. For those who have not encountered it, the argument of the book's contributors is that national traditions are invented, and are, therefore, false, conceivably a false consciousness to use the orthodox Marxist terminology. Hobsbawm, it will be recalled was a life-long communist and never seemed to have any problem with the mass killing that communism perpetrated, but let that pass. The underlying thinking of the book is not that all history is invented, perish the thought, but that the national past and its rituals, its remembrance, are made up by self-serving elites. The real stuff is class, material conditions and economic relations. Pretty orthodox Marxist stuff, really, but it resonated with the left of the time, struggling as it was to find a way out of the quagmire that the Soviet Union and the other communist states were in, and it was equally popular with the universalists, the single humanity collectivity.

What this *tendance* either failed to recognise or just ignored was that all history is subject to "invention" in the sense that the book was using it. There is no mention in the book of social construction theory, although Berger and Luckman had published their *Social Construction of Reality* in 1966 and I have no idea whether any of the contributors to the volume were aware of it. Frankly, I doubt it. Historians steer clear of social theory, not surprisingly, after all the last thing they would want to acknowledge is that what they are doing is just inventing the past, though that happens to be case. But to have accepted the social constructionist argument would have brought into question the entire project and that includes the Marxist version of history, notably that history has a message and a purpose, that there is such a thing as progress (probably "Progress"), that the deity of the left is real.

The interesting aspect of the inventor school is that its members never applied the principle to other areas, only to the national past, which rather gives the game away – it was and remains a political, at any rate an ideological project. There is nothing wrong with this as long as we come clean about it (as I have tried to do in this writing). Nevertheless, as I noted, invention certainly resonated, and generations of nationalism students were spellbound by it and by the idea of elite manipulation. All this had its charms, of course, they were only graduate students, in the midst of learning, so they could be forgiven a number of serious flaws.

One of these was that neither the historians nor the graduate students could see that they were following a fashion. Ok, we all do this from time to time, but rather less pardonable was that if one credits elite manipulation, then one should also ask the question, why was it that people by the million were ready to respond? Were they just dumb? That seems to me to be as elitist as one can be. The question was seldom answered along the lines that national identities offered people a sense of belonging to a transcendental whole, implying that they accepted national identities as real and not as invented. The cat is making merry among the pigeons.

If one forgives graduate students, doing the same with fully grown historians is somewhat more problematical. I attended a conference in The Netherlands in the late 1980s and heard a Dutch historian speak about national history in the most orthodox Hobsbawmian terms, that all these national pasts were inventions and that was it. I made myself very unpopular by saying that he was suffering from Hobsbawmitis, but that it was curable, that invention – construction – only worked if there was already something in the national past with which people could identify. Thus for the Dutch seafaring was instantly recognisable as a key part of their history, but it would not have got him very far with Hungarians. I don't think that I've ever seen anyone quite so flabbergasted as he was. I hope he has forgiven me, I was rather cruel in not resisting the temptation to be witty at his expense. But the point stands. There are limits to construction.

An even more egregious example appeared in a book that I had to review in the 1990s (I am drawing a veil over its details), in which the editor claimed that nations in Europe (she was American) were "fictive", like living in a novel I suppose. Quite apart from her being unable to tell the difference between "fictive" and "fictitious" (at least, I think that that was what she had intended to say), the woman in question had obviously no idea of social construction theory or, for that matter, that structurally the United States and all its being were as "fictive" as anything else she cared to name. Really, the dictates of intellectual fashions can be a pain in the neck. It can frivolously be compared to an aspect of the 1960s when suddenly all the girls had to wear miniskirts; in the case of studying nations and nationhood, everything had to be "invented". So, yet again, where be objectivity now, poor Yorick?

Besides, the anti-national(ist) project does not really work. However much nationhood is unmasked as invented, unreal, an elite manipulation, it has not gone away (as hoped), but keeps acquiring a new lease of life. In terms of scholarly activity, it would maybe preferable to accept it as a successful construction to investigate from that perspective. That, in sum, is what can be derived from sociology, that realities are constructed and are lived as real, however much elites of left and right, I would like to stress the *and* here, may struggle to get people to accept their exclusive definition of reality. A coda. I have added the "right" here, because nationalist historians do something similar to the left. They seek to delegitimate the histories of their nationalist, usually neighbouring, competitors. Structurally there is nothing to choose between left and right here, however much both may hate me for saying so.

In truth, all historians are as much in the business of constructing memory regimes, particular ways of recalling the past, as those whom they disdain. It all comes down to accepting one's contingency, to the impossibility of writing a total past (what a thoroughly abhorrent idea), hence the imperative of selection, which in turn raises the question of selection criteria and there we are, back in the garden of the double hermeneutic. C'est la vie.

My rather negative attitude to historians as sketched in the foregoing is primarily focused on those who see the past as a series of events, corresponding to Braudel's *histoire événementielle*, which he (rightly to my mind) criticised as skating on the surface of things.

"An incredible number of dice, always rolling, dominate and determine each individual existence: uncertainty, then in the realm of individual history; but in that of collective history ... simplicity and consistency. History is indeed 'a poor little conjectural science' when it selects individuals as its objects ... but much more rational in its procedures and results, when it examines groups and repetitions."

Braudel is quoted here by Franco Moretti in his *Graphs, Maps, Trees.* I haven't checked the original French, but I would hazard a guess that both are using "science" in the sense of knowledge, maybe "knowledge rationally pursued", rather than the English which generally restricts "science" to the natural sciences and thereby focus the social sciences on a pointless positivism, the realm of you-know-which-beastie.

There is, to be sure, the need for the kind of history that arranges the past in a series, constructs a chronological structure to create clarity in order to allow the individual and collectivity to recognise their pasts. The trouble is that too often history tends to stop there and to ignore the multiple reality of the past, a reality that can only be grasped, albeit partially, by using the manifold intellectual resources through which we try to understand the present.

Here once more I am making a plea for uncovering the past by whatever disciplinary instruments are there, have been created. If we accept that contemporary societies are successfully explored through the application of the insights of sociology and social psychology, then why not do the same with the past? Why not indeed. Surely even the most hardhat, facts-are-all historian is aware that one of the central driving forces of human activity is the quest for and use of power, in which case a theory of power should be an essential part of the historian's intellectual furniture. It seldom is, though Guglielmo Ferrero must be judged an exception. Similarly, even accepting that the study of documents is the primary legitimate activity of the historian (a big "even" as far as I'm concerned), the historian should be aware of the contingent nature of the document in question and should, at the very least, have some idea of semiotics, of being trained to interrogate a text, including the ability to assess the absence of factors that should be there, but are not. The analogy here is the French concept of *en carence*, something that should logically be there, but is absent. This multiple approach to interrogating a text further means that as far as possible, the historian should not concern himself with the personality of the writer and not take it for granted that what is written is all there is. The text has to be complemented by the metatext. And finally, the historian has to play fair with the reader and make his and her intellectual provenance clear, like whether he or she has read into the social sciences or not and if not, why not. But all this is crying for the moon.

The past of others, therefore, can often be an even worse example of the way in which historians seek to exercise power over the past. For one, the world abroad is very different, requires a major act of sociological, not just historical imagination and may well be incomprehensible. The translation function of the historian is seldom recognised as such, yet even when he is dealing with his own history, or with what he thinks is his own history, he runs the risk of deceiving the reader as translations can do, but especially if the historian plays the objectivity card. The past cannot be recovered in full, there will always be selection issues, and will always be seen through a glass darkly; besides, some glasses will be significantly darker than others. (Yes, I know, I'm deliberately conflating glass and glasses for effect. Just in case.) The best history is about making the glass as light as is feasible, because by doing so we can glimpse the difference between foxes and hedgehogs, as well as much else of course. But even the wiliest of foxes are unreliable as narrators, whilst the hedgehog won't even admit that she's a narrator at all.

When it comes to other cultures, it has not been unknown for historians to apply a different standard to their own past and to that of others. I have never ceased to be amazed at the cavalier way in which a historian will occasionally write about the past of a country of which he doesn't even know the language or at best barely. It is perfectly possible for someone to write at length about a Central European country without knowing its language and be treated as a serious scholar. But can we imagine someone writing about the US without knowing English? I was once asked to referee an article that compared Hungary, Serbia and the Czech Republic, and the author knew none of the languages. It was full of misunderstandings and mistranslations – the author used only English language materials – and its argument was poor stuff. I sent it back, recommending a rejection. The editors chose to ignore my reasoning and published it. It's a neat example of an uneven power relationship and of the failure of the historian as translator. Heaven alone knows what the readers of the journal made of it. Cancelled their subscriptions, I hope.

It should be clear enough from the foregoing that I am firmly of the view that historians will always have baggage of their own, that this necessarily affects what and how they write about the past and, therefore, they should just forget about objectivity. If only historians were ready to admit that theirs is just one possible version of the past, that it is their construction – theirs and that of the memory regime in which they live, move and have their being, not to mention embarrassing factors like the approval of their colleagues, the need for tenure, the pressure to publish for the sake of research assessors, the better their readers would be served. I also know, however, that the structures of academic life make this plea of mine pretty pointless. Academia is as full of tares as in The Bible and my argument is affected by the reality that I do not have to publish or perish. Too old and out of that particular rat race.

Beyond all the above is the very hard question of what history is actually for. Memory regimes are one thing, fair enough, but what is it that motivates the historian? I don't for one moment believe that there is such a thing as history as it really was, *wie es eigentlich gewesen*, to recall von Ranke's words, for all the reasons adduced here, nor do I seriously think that anything in the universe is *sine ire et studio*, if we interpret *ire* as generously as it may be, to include a wide range of emotions, not just anger. Nor is it true, I venture to suggest, that "those who cannot remember the past are condemned to repeat it". It sounds good, Santayana often does, but if we interrogate the quote, does it stand up?

History, yes, actually tells us otherwise. Here is an obvious example. The leadership of the United States knew full well that foreign invasions of Afghanistan invariably fail (well, have done so hitherto). The three British-Afghan wars were testimony enough, but the defeat of the Soviet Union was very recent indeed and brought about in part by US help. Yet what does George Bush II do? Invades Afghanistan. It beggars belief, but it happened. Or, another example with greater historical distance. Napoleon invaded Russia and was defeated. The factors are well known – the impossible supply lines, the climate, the Russians' scorched earth policy. Hitler does the same thing. Learning from history? No way.

So let's put these three well-worn quotes to one side and ask another question. What is it that makes the European tradition of history writing different? First, it has been separated from a divine purpose, although the Hegelians made a fairly good job of recreating purposiveness by the invention of the spirit of history. The spirit of progress is not far away from purposiveness and even election by History. I'm deeply sceptical, but then that's me. Second, it claims to be scientific and objective, evidently a way of differentiating modern history from the pre-modern. Third, the historian is not there to serve a political master (*pace* research assessment), but is autonomous.

Take another puzzling case. The facts of a particular event in the past are, let us say, agreed by two historians, yet the conclusions they draw from those facts are diametrically the opposite. Does this mean that one of them is objective and the other a charlatan? If so, a new problem arises, what are the criteria and who selects them? And does this selection remain constant or does it change over time? Difficult, yet there is a clear-cut example of it. Zawodny's history of the 1944 Warsaw Uprising is entitled *Nothing but Honour*, which is a thesis in itself. Jan Ciechanowski, in his *The Warsaw Rising of 1944*, on the other hand, saw the Uprising as wholly irresponsible because it brought about terrible destruction and the loss of life. It adds piquancy to the dilemma that both the authors had participated in the Uprising. From my perspective, these two very different conclusions about an event in the past are perfectly proper and reflect the values of the authors, which are evidently incommensurable, but that plays ducks and drakes with any concept of historical objectivity.

However, if I'm right so far, we can forget the ostensible aims of historians and try to pierce the veil. I would like to suggest the following motives, not by any means conscious ones. Together with all who toil in the vineyard, historians do so because they want to add something to the sum total of human knowledge, which is perfectly respectable as far as I am concerned. Then, historians being human want recognition, again nothing reprehensible in that. Third, they may want simply to entertain their readers – certainly the popular historians disliked by the profession do so. Career reasons come into it as well.

But whatever historians may think about what they are doing, history *qua* history has to be assessed by deeper criteria (mine). The past may be a storehouse of exemplars to be followed or not à la Santayana, but above all it legitimates the present, it legitimates power, it offers a discourse by which current actions are explained and made acceptable. Historians, by writing a particular version of the past, create the cognitive framework into which these discursive initiatives can be fitted. I'm not suggesting that historians are no more than the handmaidens of power, though there are examples of that too, but every society has to have a sense of its own past (as well as of its future) and that past structures the present.

Conversely, the present structures the way in which we understand the past and imposes obligations on the historian to write about the past in ways that were not regarded as necessary in the past. Think of the way in which the historians have turned towards the marginal, the dispossessed, the oppressed as a means of legitimating their present position in society and/or delegitimating the claims of the majority. Fashion rules or something; the current focus on (take your pick) the history of the Atlantic slave trade is a good illustration. The Arab slaving past in East Africa does not have this attention.

History, therefore, is a very different enterprise from what the historians would have us believe. They need to satisfy their professionalism and, who knows, their sponsors, that they are writing something scientific, objective and *sub specie aeternitatis*. The possibility that they are only writing to sustain some particular segment of the tribe is too awful to contemplate, even if this what we – we humans – actually do all the time. There is no central, global, universal history, each of us is a captive of our local, particular, dare I add national pasts and that is what we conjure up when writing about. Generally we have a message of some kind, and this is perfectly legitimate as long as we understand that this what the exercise is about. All humans are normative, involved in value creation, so why not historians? Those who claim that historians are special in their ability to reflect the past neutrally are deceiving themselves and their readers. What they can do, do in fact do, is to reflect a particular bit of the past that is thought to be relevant to contemporary issues. Fine, legitimating one's argument by reference to antiquity, to tradition, to precedent is a standard device in European culture. Note here that if a historian's argument goes counter to the hegemonic belief system, it will just be screened out, ignored or, at best, regarded as "mad, bad and dangerous to know".

This last can, however, be of enormous significance when it comes to evaluating the different histories of different collectivities. Doing so shows up that the histories of the winners are very different from those of the losers or even that of large states against small states. Norman Davies caused a stir with his *The Isles*, a history of the British Isles which treated Scottish, Irish and Welsh history as equal to that of the English. Notably, that when the English executed Charles I in 1649, it didn't seem to occur to them that they were also beheading the King of Scotland. And if we look at the history of the 20th century, the histories of the smaller states are duly ignored. Thus the Portuguese contribution to the First World War is unknown, the German and Austro-Hungarian fighting against Russia, like the Siege of Przemyśl, the breakthrough at Gorlice, the Brusilov offensive are unknown to the obsessives of the history of the Western front, seen as the real First World War. Attempts to widen the scope of history beyond the canon are pretty hopeless, because the cognitive framing is well and truly in place and can only be changed over time by considerable effort, energy and money.

Historians will usually deny that there is such a thing as a canon at all, it's ok in literature, but they are above that sort if thing, because they are in search of the Truth. This may be so, but it's not truth with a capital, but a particular dimension of their own collective past. All history will reflect the concerns of the present, the legitimation of these concerns and the cohesion of the collectivity by confirming it and/or denying it. All this means is that writing history is about underpinning collective agency and the collective self. This has deeper consequences. If a state or nation can endow itself with a successful past, then it will generally be insensitive to the rather more troubled pasts of others. A large part of the history of the states and nations of Central Europe is about loss of agency, the absolute loss rather too often to be comfortable about the present. In a word, these states have very different pasts and memory regimes when compared with Britain and France. Unless this loss of agency is recognised and accepted by larger actors, the smaller ones will be constantly uneasy with elements of ressentiment, injustice, indeterminacy will keep breaking through, much to the irritation of the larger entities.

It may well be that the practitioners of *histoire croisée*, somewhat idiosyncratically Englished as "entangled history", should be exempt from my strictures. The little that I've read suggests that they are looking at the interconnections that mark the past. I would have to do more work to be certain, but I would like to make a very tentative guess that these *historiens croisés* (crossed historians? hm) don't seem to appreciate that all systems of power seek to condense meanings, to claim a single monological variant of the past, the one that legitimates them of course, so that when all's said and done, all history writing is imperfect, as are the humans involved, precisely because they are humans and not the inhabitants of Planet Plato (no, not a misreading for Pluto). To add a further thought, some of these *croisiers*, (to coin another term, or should that be *croisistes* or *croisards*?), are anti-nationalists and universalists. Is that superior in some obscure way?

None of this should be taken to mean that I don't enjoy reading history, on the contrary. Some historical accounts definitely come into category of being "a good read". I was spellbound by Christopher Clark's *Sleepwalkers*, for example. And I have enormous respect for the strict methodology insisted on by Jenő Szűcs, to my mind the most outstanding Hungarian historian of the twentieth century. They add to one's store of information and may even enlarge one's cultural capital, or maybe serve as ammunition in debate. The single instance precedent will often convince people, though it really shouldn't, unless one is a devotee of the principle that one should only ever generalise from one case, because a second one may disturb the argument. This is something that historians seldom acknowledge, that their generalisations may be decidedly weakly grounded and will be vulnerable to the single exception, the Black Swan proposition. Hence Popper's insistence that falsification is stronger ground than verification in advancing assertions. But accepting that would seduce historians from the rules of their game and make them outcasts by other members of the guild.

After 1945: Cold War, Cold Peace[*]

Why did the attempts to establish peace after WW1 fail? How was this different from after WW2? Why was peacemaking concluded in the particular form that it took, in other words what were the contingent circumstances that shaped the attitudes of those who took the policy decisions? And how did they understand the other players? In other words, I put the stress on chance, accident, happenstance and, it may be, human frailty, on the fallibility of knowledge, on the interpretation of precedent and on unintended consequences. Linear thinking, that B followed A, hence there is a causal nexus between the two, is a classic example of error. Assumptions of linearity are deeply coded in Western thinking.

There was terrible loss of life in WW1, but this was mostly military; the civilian population, affected only where there was direct fighting, was not targeted. Besides, on the Western front, the fighting was static, thereby sparing the civilian population. On the Italian front, the fighting took place in a relatively narrow area, whilst the civilians on the Eastern front were not a part of anyone's focus. WW2 was different, though fewer soldiers were killed, civilian deaths and urban destruction were horrendous. Hence the imperative to eliminate war from European history was far stronger than after 1918.

There was a learning process. The Paris Peace Settlement was about revenge, maximising one's security by adding territory, about disman-

---

* This chapter is an edited version of my contribution to the launch of Mihály Fülöp's book, *The Unfinished Peace: the Council of Foreign Ministers and the Hungarian Peace Treaty of 1947* at the Hungarian Academy of Sciences, 3 May 2013.

tling the landward empires of the east (to ensure that they would never again threaten the victorious allies); to that can be added war guilt and reparations (*Kriegsschuld* is both), there was no attempt to plan for reconciliation and the Western allies, the victors had no real conception of how the new states that they brought into being would function as states. The mental model was the slow dismantling of the Ottoman empire in the 19th century, but no one really cared about the semi-functional cases that came into being. After WW2, things were different, partly because the motives were different (the destruction was on a different quality and scale), partly because the Paris Peace Settlement model was seen to have failed (evidently).

The process of modernity was far from complete in 1914, by 1945 it was largely – not wholly finished – the conversion of peasants into citizens and the corresponding enlargement of the public sphere. The two wars accelerated this process. This subsequently gave democracy a different quality from the interwar period, by diffusing power. Modernity here also means completing the process of ending primary poverty – insufficient food, heat, light, shelter. For much of Europe this process lasted well into the 1960s.

Peace was easier to make in 1947, because it did not really have Central and South-Eastern Europe to bother with. The region was under Soviet control, for many in the West this was a stabilising process, an attitude that lasted throughout the communist period. And even now is seen in some quarters with an element of nostalgia. The trouble is that Western Europe has never really taken the trouble to learn what it is that makes Europe east of Elbe tick.

There was and is an element of disdain towards Central and South-Eastern Europe in this. The two world wars both had their casus belli in the region and post hoc operated as propter hoc, causation is frequently attributed on this flawed basis. For many this became a good reason to put the region into cold storage, Central and South-Eastern Europe being given their statehood was seen tacitly somehow as a historic error. The cold storage metaphor reemerged shortly after 1989.

There were further lessons learned from the interwar period. First, populations could be moved en masse, forcibly if need be or exterminated or ethnically cleansed for the purpose of establishing mono-ethnic, homogeneous states – mono-ethnicity was seen as a stabilising factor. The experience of the League of Nations with the nationalities issue was central in this. The fact that this was a copy of Nazi methods troubled no one. Then, despite the Paris Peace Settlement, while "guilt" was redefined as "war criminality", thus a matter of individual rather collective action, nevertheless victorious and defeated states were treated differently. The former got their territories back (Alsace-Lorraine), the latter had to live with losing territory, whether these were gained in WW2 or as a result of WW1 (Italy). Poland both lost and gained. Bulgaria, though on the defeated side, actually gained territory. Hungary lost what it had acquired in 1938–1941 and even lost the Bratislava bridgehead. Czechoslovakia lost Subcarpathian Ruthenia, which could have been a gain.

There was another tacit principle in operation. The shapes of states could change, but no new states could come into being (unlike 1918). The Baltic states, having been swallowed by the Soviet Union, stayed swallowed.

Even more important was the proposition that the arrangement and configuration of states now arrived at what was to be regarded as permanent, if not actually immanent. States, therefore, were no longer to be seen as products of history, but were sacralised in their existing form as supratemporal and, equally, as supraspatial. Helsinki finalised this as between West and East. German reunification was the one exception, or was intended to be. Clio does not like to be fettered.

With a few exceptions, decolonisation could not and would not apply to Europe, even where the power relationship between metropole and region was colonial or semi-colonial. Cyprus, Malta and Ireland were the exceptions, though Iceland also falls into this category. Colonial or excolonial status has not been extended to the former subject territories of the landward empires of Europe and that includes the Soviet Union. True, they have not really sought it and the former overseas imperial states have enough post-colonial guilt to worry about anyway. Yet in the post-1991 world, where victimhood and victimhood competition play a vital role, the demand for ex-colonial status could have brought considerable advantages, even if it would have been immensely complex in some cases, with double and triple colonisations.

The idea of Europe was reconfigured thanks to the recognition that only by reincorporating Germany and working hard to sustain the Paris-Bonn axis as its centre could the Europe of the Cold Peace be brought into being. No more *Erbfeindschaft*, therefore. Note that the absence of Franco-German competition over Central Europe, something that had bedevilled the region in the interwar years, was a helpful condition in this process – the dividend of the Cold Peace, one might say.

Then, the new Europe was committed to democracy. This proposition was not so self-evident in 1950 as it is today. In the 1930s authoritarian systems were seen as normal and dynamic. Somewhere there emerged the proposition that democracy makes war impossible. The UK chose to stay outside this system, found itself obliged to accept the newly constructed power centre on the Continent, but then did what it could to prevent it from converting its economic power into political power.

In this new Europe, state sovereignty remains, but some of that sovereignty has been transferred to Brussels voluntarily, or mostly so. Compare here the Brezhnev doctrine of limited sovereignty proclaimed in the aftermath of the invasion of Czechoslovakia in 1968. The EU is, in this sense, functioning on the basis of a limited sovereignty, but it is different from Brezhnev's variant in that it is consensual, albeit small states have only a limited choice about falling into line. Ideally, the trade-off is that by acceding to this EU version of limited sovereignty, they gain something – the relationship between them and large powers is now properly regulated. Again, this can be regarded as one of the benefits of the Cold Peace.

The European integration process, therefore, became skilled in conflict resolution, not least in the EU Commission operated as the defender of the interests of the smaller states and developed consensual modes of domesticating power (István Bibó wrote of "taming" power). Over the years these processes and procedures came to work well, but they were not really adjusted to include the new members of the EU which joined after 2004. Political cultures are difficult to adapt to new situations. Furthermore, conflict resolution was disturbed by the power accumulating in the EU and the growing autonomy of the Commission as an autonomous site of power that increasingly questioned the status and sovereignty of the member states.

The number of inter-state relations to be managed was relatively small – the proliferation of new states after 1918 was much disliked – hence in the West much revolved around the relationship between France and Germany. Scandinavia opted for a trade relationship with the UK, the Mediterranean dictatorships only rejoined Europe in the 1970s. The absence of Central and South-Eastern Europe in a way helped the coming into being of a "civilised" Europe, Western Europe, without the hairy barbarians to the east. Indeed, for 45 years Europe had a negative other, an alterity, to the east and this was extremely helpful in consolidating the very particular Europe that was being constructed by the Monnet method. The formation of Europe that was brought into being from the 1950s onwards and the European identity that was constructed around it are the evidence. The Cold Peace was, on this argument, a very helpful condition indeed to the European integration process and the emergence of the new Europe, though it is hard to decide whether or not it was a necessary condition.

Was the 1947 peace-making a steppingstone towards the Cold War? Only in part, in that it made few gestures towards reconciliation between former enemies (these were early days), but did attempt to close a longue durée chapter of European history, that of territorial rearrangement after a war. There is no question in my mind that the absolute conservatism of the US towards territorial rearrangement, as well as the looming presence of the Soviet Union, were at the back of this, presumably in the belief that definitive frontiers promote stability. In political reality, this conservatism shifts a possible political fault line from the international to the domestic political arena, where in general majorities are strong enough to keep down transfrontier minorities or they do a deal (Belgium, Netherlands). Note that as the concept and practice of democracy evolved – an ever wider public sphere and the acceptance of minority action in politics (some minorities only), proliferating forms of representation – the conditions of territorial stability require a good deal more accommodation than once upon time.

The 45 years of peace, however, the unintended child of the 1947 Peace Treaties, did have a consequence that few ever even conceived of at the time – the division of Europe left the West entirely without knowledge and experience of Central Europe. Hence the EU had no idea what to do with states that have had an utterly different history – the Mediterranean dictatorships were not a good model – and which have agendas of their own at odds with deep-rooted Western assumptions. In particular, the states of the region were much less stable territorially, all had been subordinated to one empire or another in a colonial or semi-colonial relationship; correspondingly the nation in its ethnic dimension became the guarantor of the collectivity; and given that serfdom persisted into the 19th century, the solution of the peasant question posed entirely different demands.

Nor did the West understand – couldn't? wouldn't? – the dehumanising quality of communist rule. The putative coming together of Europe after 1989 and 1991 coincided with the euphoria of the victory over communism, the "end of history", the unipolar moment, the US as hyperpower and a corresponding disdain for difference, not major difference, but enough minor differences to cause irritation. Central Europe just won't conform and the West refuses to apply the rules of multiculturalism to Central Europe. The reason, presumably, is that doing so would threaten the West's own assumptions, its own narratives, its universalist aspirations and the worldwide validity of whatever the West decrees. This source of friction, again a consequence of the Cold Peace, will run and run.

Central Europe:
Kundera, Incompleteness, Lack of Agency*

It is hard to avoid returning to Milan Kundera when reflecting on Central Europe. This is hardly surprising as he ended up more or less reinventing the concept with his "Kidnapped Europe" essay of 1983, also entitled "The Tragedy of Central Europe". And a thoroughly reluctant reinventor he proved to be, almost as if he was fearful or ashamed of having relaunched Central Europe on its post-Yalta career. Yalta was thought to end Central Europe, as the result of the very hard division of Europe between eastern and western sections, something that was most acutely visible in Berlin, which before the building of the Wall was marked out by boundary markers warning, "you are leaving the US sector". The Wall made the division more visible yet.

So let us go back in time a bit. What's in a name, cried Shakespeare's Juliet, and the answer, unlike hers, is that it can be a great deal indeed. If Yalta came to be the ultimate symbol of division, this separation of Europe into western and eastern parts fairly quickly acquired ethical connotations. The western was the "good" part and the east was the "bad", the West's shadow or dark brother, as it were. This had the effect of sealing the division for a very long time. And it was a source of comfort for the West that however many errors it may have committed, however much the burden of the colonial past rested heavy on the post-imperi-

---

* An edited version of the chapter first published in Leonidas Donskis (ed.), *Yet Another Europe after 1984: Rethinking Milan Kundera and the Idea of Central Europe* (Amsterdam: Rodopi, 2012), 1730.

al states, at least the West was superior in being democratic. Note that in some respects this pride was not unjustified. The integration of Europe along the lines laid out by Jean Monnet and Altiero Spinelli worked – there is peace and democracy firmly entrenched, much more so than anyone would have thought in 1945. All the same, having the dark brother to the east was helpful; indeed, Stalin could be regarded as one of the unintentional founding fathers of the EU. This necessarily meant that Europe – a rump Europe to be sure – did not have to think about Central Europe or of whether those Europeans who had been absorbed by the Soviet Union were a loss to Europe. The founding fathers of European integration had left the question of Central and South-Eastern Europe open. Western Europe, now the sole remaining claimant to the title of being European, mostly looked the other way.

So for several post-Yalta decades, the word "Europe" referred to Western Europe only, having air-brushed the rest out of time and space and in a tacit sense, the non-democratic states of the West (Spain, Portugal, Greece) were not quite inside the definition either. Everything to the east of the Iron Curtain was Eastern Europe, a term that could or could not include the Soviet Union. General de Gaulle may have spoken of Europe from the Atlantic to the Urals, but his wish-fulfilment fantasy of including Russia in a Gaullist Europe remained just that, beyond the pale – literally in this case, given the hard, physical quality of the barbed wire and minefields. In truth, the term Eastern Europe was rather crude – shorthand terms often have this quality – driven as it was by political criteria and went against geography, history and culture (as politics frequently can do). But, of course, as the politics changed, so did the definition of Europe.

What gave the impulse to this change was most likely the Helsinki Final Act, which was supposed to stabilise Europe in its western and eastern guises, but contributed to the eventual demise of communism thanks to the introduction of the institution of human rights into communist systems as a reference point external to Marxism-Leninism. By the 1980s, an interesting gap had opened up between West European and US usage. For the latter, "Europe" was Western Europe only. For the former, Europe increasingly included the countries to the east of the Elbe and there was quiet disagreement about whether or not Russia was inside Europe. Of course, at the time hardly anyone dreamed of the collapse of communism, the end of Soviet domination and the disintegration of communist federations (Soviet Union, Yugoslavia, Czechoslovakia) with the consequent emergence of new-old Central European states, but Europe was quietly undergoing enlargement all the same. Americans, obdurate devotees of the status quo where state stability is concerned, were decidedly slow to recognise the changes that Helsinki had wrought.

This was the context into which Kundera cast the stone that put so much to flight, himself included as it turned out. In a very real sense, he seized the moment and proved capable of concentrating a feeling, giving form to an atmosphere intuitively, to the effect that Central Europe, whatever that was, could be reemerging on the European stage. Which stage that was unclear – political, economic, cultural, social, literary could all be defined and indeed were, albeit with decidedly fuzzy and contested parameters. It is more than likely that it was this contest that frightened Kundera, especially the attacks he received for suggesting that Russia was outside Central Europe and possibly Europe itself. In sum, Kundera was shocked by having exercised agency. The problem of agency and Central Europe will form a vital part of this essay.

Certainly, having grasped a mood that became a fashion and then something like bandwagon – large numbers of articles were devoted to the topos in the second half of the 1980s – Kundera withdrew from the fray entirely and would have nothing to do with any thought of republishing his essay. A personal anecdote follows. When Nancy Wood and I undertook to edit the book that became *In Search of Central Europe*, we were certain that Kundera would let us republish his text. An enormous mistake. I wrote to him, asking for permission, explaining that this was to be a serious, academic, scholarly work and one of great importance thanks to him (one lays it on, on such occasions). I no longer have the correspondence, it got lost somewhere when I moved from London, but from memory, I received a curt no, in French. Well, nothing ventured, nothing gained, I thought, and penned an even more obsequious letter. The answer came a few days later in the form of an aggressive telephone call from his British publishers, that if we went ahead, Kundera, the publisher and everyone else would sue me forever and a day. So, we gave up on the idea and made do with a summary of Kundera's argument that was well within fair dealing and scholarly ground rules. I never heard from Kundera again, so most probably he never saw the book and, therefore, felt safe that his honour, safety, reputation, whatever had not been impugned.

But whatever Kundera's personal problems, once the text was in the public domain, it could not be withdrawn. It was published first in French and then in English in *Granta* and then the *New York Review of Books*. Other languages followed, including samizdat in all probability. So copies of it are around and it can be said to have a semi-covert existence. It is widely known, but difficult though not impossible to find, which is simultaneously liberating and irritating, because anyone can use ideas from it, but can't readily check what Kundera actually wrote. (There is a version on the internet, see the bibliography for the link.)

A number of propositions can be advanced, which have their origins in the Kundera insight. The first of these is that Central Europe does have a distinct existence. What the form and content of that separate identity actually consists of is very much open to debate. More or less everyone who has laboured in this vineyard has his and her definition, and that includes me. Clearly, in the essay Kundera was concerned to delegitimate communism and the Russian imperial project, which was aimed at giving these countries or, better, cultures an ineradicable Russian content, thereby tying them somehow to Mother Russia. This project failed with the cultures, though it certainly succeeded with a goodly number of individuals. But cultures resist the coercive imposition of norms perceived to be alien.

Lenin, Stalin and their successors could have had no knowledge of postcolonial theory, but even they must have had some intimation that coercive universalisation would generate resistance – much of the history of the Soviet Union shows nothing less. Lenin's slogan, "national in form, socialist in content" was based on the assumption that form really did not matter, that the socialist content would always trump national form. This is simply not true. But coercive transformations are very much a part of the longue durée history of Central Europe, so the inherited collective knowledge certainly includes traditions of saying, "we resist, we will withstand you". I can still remember a conversation with the Hungarian writer, the late Miklós Mészöly, in the 1960s, when I asked him about the post-1956 Soviet presence. "We had the Turks in Hungary for 150 years," he replied, "and who speaks Turkish there now?" A collection of the writings of Mihály Babits, the Hungarian poet and writer, was published under the title "Légy ellenállás", which translates as "Be resistance!" (except that given the ambiguity of language, it could also be "The resistance of flies").

One of the key qualities of Central Europe, then, is its experience – its repeated experience – of externally derived and constructed transformations. I have analysed this in detail in my *Dilemmas of Identity*, so I will not repeat the argument in this place, other than to provide a list: feudalism, Reformation, Counter-Reformation, Enlightenment, modernity, independent statehood, modern nationhood, fascism, communism, mass population movement. What is striking about these attempts at transformation is that they produced something other than what the external power sought to attain, an incompleteness, an unsatisfactory hybrid between elements of the transformative project and the local tradition. At the same time, the repeated ignoring by the external transformers of the local tradition produced a sense of loss of agency – weakness of agency too had become a part of the incompleteness.

Poles, Czechs, Hungarians all have their moments of absolute non-agency, when exogamous power imposed a solution that was brutal, supposedly definitive and irreversible. For Poland, this was the four partitions; for the Czechs it was the aftermath of the Battle of White Mountain in 1618 and then Munich (1938); for the Hungarians, it was the Treaty of Trianon in 1920. The memory of these events has never quite disappeared, but lives on in ghostly form as the humiliation of helplessness. On an everyday level, of course, people do not go around musing on these events, but their offstage role is incontestably a part of their reality structures.

All this will be familiar to students of postcolonial theory and the long term outcome of colonialism. Colonies are generally supposed to exist outside Europe, so the thought that there may be landward colonies inside Europe is rejected by many. They attribute full agency to Central Europe and, therefore, persist with their transformative activities and regard resistance as reactionary or retrogressive or just plain obstinacy. The postulate that Central Europeans may be seeking their own models of modernity that can indeed differ from those of a real or putative West is simply ignored. There is no real structural difference here between Joseph II's attempt to impose German on his realm (in the name of progress) and Western environmentalists insisting that Central Europeans follow their recipes without questioning them (likewise).

If one examines the relationship between Western and Central Europe without the blinkers that deny forms of colonialism within Europe, then many of the tropes of a colonial type dependency can readily be discerned, quite apart from areas that really were incorporated into one empire or another – in the 19th century Western Poland, for one, was clearly exposed to Germanisation and suffered doubly from Bismarck's anti-Catholic Kulturkampf (the original one) as well.

The repeated reproduction of this process, then, can be seen as a key element in the Central European experience. The exercise of alien power (Hapsburg, German, Russian, Turkish, Reformation, Counter-Reformation), which begins from alien assumptions generates similar outcomes – the subordinate, the subaltern can never become like the alien moderniser, cannot undergo a complete identity shift, hence the incompleteness. But this has a consequence. Because the projects remain incomplete in Central Europe, this shows up these projects as being just that, as projects, as forms of naturalised knowledge on the part of the alien transformer. Crucially, this brings intro relief the universalism of

Western modernity and legitimates resistance to it, so that the modernisers will do what they can via discursive techniques to present resistance as reactionary obscurantism and not as the legitimate defence of local values. The clash of legitimating discourses has had a far-reaching impact on Central Europe, not least in bringing into being comprador representatives of the external power, just as Marx described in the case of overseas colonies. (Peiker)

One illustration of this type of clash was that in the 1990s, there gradually evolved a proposition (the use of the impersonal is deliberate, there was no obvious agency) that the West had put nationalism behind it and had become post-national. Note: this was and remains an assertion, no evidence is marshalled to support it. Crucially, in the West, so this argumentation went, ethnicity was no more, it had somehow evaporated and only Third World immigrants and their descendants had a benign ethnic identity. This normative proposal was at the root of the disappearance of the words "state" and "country" and their replacement by the now defanged "nation", which of course was never, but never nationalistic, at most it would pursue the national interest.

Then along come these tiresome Central Europeans and argue in favour of their own identities and values, which could be seriously at variance with what the West regarded as proper and thereby questioned the entire Western project. In addition, in Central Europe, state, nation and ethnicity were not co-terminous, seeing that there were minorities and the frontiers which the West – or some in the West – had repeatedly recast were in consequence seen by some as supposedly soft and, therefore, a source of danger. An illustration: during the 1990s, American journalists repeatedly warned of an inter-ethnic war between Romania and Hungary over Transylvania; the fact that this never happened deterred none of them – such is the discreet charm of the freedom of the media. In reality both after the first and the second world wars, the Western powers imposed extensive frontier changes and population shifts, often to satisfy their client states (like Czechoslovakia) without for a second stopping to ask the people involved what they might have wanted.

Messengers bringing bad news are seldom welcome and this is especially so when the bad news places a question mark over one's own sense of virtue. So has it been with Central Europe's impact on Europe as a whole, whether before the eastward enlargement of the EU or afterwards.

Yet there is more to it all than meets the eye. One of Kundera's key insights is that Central Europe functions as Europe's early warning system. He drew this conclusion, intuitively I think, from Kafka's depiction of soulless and meaningless bureaucracy. It is worth delving into this insight more deeply. First, the early warning system metaphor functions precisely because of the incompleteness explored above. Systems are set up and for various reasons they don't work well, hence the shortcomings of the system as such are exposed. This is what Central Europe has shown repeatedly and has thereby earned the eternal disdain of happier countries to the West. As I have noted, messengers bearing ill tidings are seldom welcome. This is all the more acute when the systemic failing can be seen as structural, rather than contingent on some local factor. The demonstration by Central Europe that nationhood is not and, indeed, cannot be only civic, but necessarily includes an ethnic element is bad news for the protagonists of post-nationalism; and it goes without saying that they blame Central Europe for showing them to be less virtuous than they think.

If one of Europe's greatest attainments has been the conversion of peasants into citizens with autonomy and agency, something that Western Europe was able to do broadly by relying on its own intellectual, moral and material resources, then Central Europe followed a different path, one that was dictated both by alien power and economic weakness. In ideal-typical terms, the process assumes the existence of a traditional peasantry reliant on patrimonial production, largely outside the market in being unable to engage with it, though affected by it (Verdery 1983). This reproduces a passivity and fatalism regarding the wider world. From this it follows that while the peasant would have knowledge of his or her immediate village surroundings (kinship, rituals, seasonal cycles), the impact of the rest of the world was inexplicable or threatening. Giv-

en widespread illiteracy, the primary source of wider knowledge was religion, meaning mostly stasis but potentially open to the sudden, overwhelming change encoded in salvation.

It is clear enough that in this model it is hard to conceptualise the traditional peasantry becoming citizens, but this is what the arrival of modernity in the form of the market and, somewhat later, literacy brought about.
Nowhere in Europe was the process painless or rapid – this incidentally is
one of the key processes that differentiates Europe from North America,
where there was no traditional peasantry, the South being a partial exception given slavery. In Western Europe, the transformation was often harsh,
but was – again broadly – achieved through local intellectual and cognitive resources. It is worth adding that the process was completed much later than widely assumed, in the 1960s and 1970s. Jacques Tati's film, *Jour
de fête* made in 1949, shows a wonderfully evocative picture of rural France
where, apart from electrification, nothing much has changed.

In Central Europe something different happened. Communism simply destroyed the peasant way of life and did so very rapidly, roughly between 1950 and 1970, through accelerated industrialisation and overr-
apid urbanisation (the Czech lands were an exception to this overall
pattern). The rural population, which was generally, though not entirely,
more marginal than their most successful counterparts in the West (like
France), was driven into urban centres. The process was harsh and, often
enough, cruel. However, there was a bargain of sorts at the centre. The
new urban working class was given a reliable material existence and the
status of worker; in exchange, he and she were expected to be passive and
to be dependent on the state, the great benefactor. This largely worked,
except when nationalism came into the picture and the newly urbanised
workers could be mobilised against an alien power (as in Berlin 1953, in
Hungary in 1956, in Czechoslovakia 1968, Poland in 1956, though in
1980 it was somewhat different).

The outcome of this near fantastical social engineering project was
the creation not of citizens, with a degree of autonomy and a sense of
agency, but a class of dependent, to some degree passive individuals, to

some extent atomised and, above all, distrustful of the state on which it depended. This picture was beginning to change by the 1980s, when a second generation of urban workers had come to maturity and took the benefits of urbanisation for granted. A personal memory from the early 1990s: standing next to me on the very long escalator at the Moszkva tér metro in Budapest (renamed since to Széll Kálmán tér) was a three generation family, consisting of granny, her daughter and grandson aged about 17. The granny dressed as a peasant in black had her eyes shut, complained the while and simply couldn't cope with something as utterly alien as a moving staircase, the daughter appeared somewhat embarrassed and was silent, while the boy – evidently a Budapest person – comforted his grandmother. For him, the escalator was the norm.

In this connection one of the striking aspects of the ideas and ideals underlying Solidarity was not just its challenge to the leading role of the party, but its commitment to collective action, egalitarianism and a high level of social and political homogeneity. Predictably, the collapse of communism did not immediately convert them into Jeffersonian democrats, but rather left them watchful, often in difficulty over decoding the new world of consumerism that had sprung up around them. They had the formal right of civic action and participation, but had to learn an entirely new set of cognitive, semantic and intellectual skills.

The argument so far has been about incompleteness being one of Central Europe's defining features. It should be understood, as has been implicit in the foregoing, that both completeness and incompleteness have a strongly subjective quality and that the ideal of completeness is measured against what Central Europeans believe to be the completeness of the West. This belief in incompleteness is then underpinned by the repeated interventions of the West or of parts of the West in the region, formerly by military means, nowadays discursively, to pressurise one or other Central European state to do something or to stop doing something that the West does not like.

The structure of this incompleteness demands further analysis, because some of it is not at all self-evident. The word implies that incomplete collectivities are lacking something that others have or are thought to have. The problem then is to identify the missing parts and then, how to complete the collective self, what to complete, which parts of the putatively completed West or of Europe (both these in the imagined or mythic sense) should be developed and which should be discarded. Again, social engineering is not far away from here. Then, once the undertaking is sketched, which it is repeatedly, the completion – again a mythic category – becomes a devastating political contest over who should have the right to set the agenda, the form and content of whatever completeness requires and how, if at all, corrections are to be implemented. This state of affairs inevitably involves the power of the state and the near impossibility of creating a neutral public function, neutral in the Weberian sense of applying rationality in the framework of the law. This situation means, further, that the quality of political action is different from that of the real or imagined West, in that it repeatedly refers back to ethical or even ontological issues that are regarded as settled elsewhere. The outcome of this contest, then, is that different social, political and sometimes religious currents in society come close to being segments, and the coherence that society seeks to attain never is, because the different segments are sufficiently rooted to secure their reproduction and, indeed, potentate each other. The overall outcome, therefore, is that Central European political activity differs from its Western counterparts, is coloured by a quest of the unattainable, engages in generally fruitless ontological projects and tries to use political power for non-political objectives, which then weaken, if not actually vitiate, democracy.

Different social categories, metamorphosed into political forces, contest the political field each with its own ontological project, to be reached by political means. And that necessarily politicises culture, which thereby lends political activity an identity-driven quality, which is, as always, extremely difficult to compromise – what suffers is democracy.

If we accept the concept of incompleteness as one of the defining features of Central Europe, then a number of issues acquire a different and, in some respects, clearer quality. Why is it, for one, that liberalism remains weak, not to say a marginal feature of the political scene, albeit it never quite disappears? And that it tends to be a phenomenon largely restricted to the capital city? The suggested explanation is that before liberalism can acquire sizeable support, there has to be confidence in one's nationhood in both its civic and ethnic dimensions, a confidence that one's nation has acquired parity of esteem abroad and the unquestioned capacity for cultural reproduction at home.

These, however, are the very features that Central Europe can never take for granted. Consequently, the universalism of liberal principles that normatively transcend the local and reach out to the whole of humanity simply never get very far. Whenever a liberal movement begins to spread its wings, it discovers that the call of the insecurity of nationhood pulls back even sympathisers. What then tends to happen is either that the liberals become yet more universalist and thereby place themselves in a minority position, in the hope presumably that society will catch up with them one day (it never does) or alternatively they become national liberals, in which event the national will mostly trump the universalism of liberalism and it will become a local-national phenomenon, and possibly quite a successful one at that.

From the perspective of their Western counterparts, however, all this is puzzling if not actually scandalous. The universalists believe in a single Europe (to be projected globally) and in as much as Central Europe fails to conform to this idealised mental model, it is seen as deviant. Deviancy of this kind must be brought back into line and pressure is then exerted on the Central Europeans to that end. But that pressure becomes a variant of the standard Western (or Eastern) attempt to impose an externally derived system of norms and thereby reproduces the phenomenon sketched in this essay.

If we accept that the consequence of incompleteness is a pervasive sense of lack of agency – note again that this is a subjective perception, but then that is what counts – then it becomes clearer why various compensatory belief systems gain traction. I have dealt at length with the phenomenon of ideological thinking in my *Dilemmas* book, but what is fascinating is how easily otherwise thoughtful individuals can, possibly through frustration, slip into conspiracy theory explanations. These explanations do have the quality of simplicity and superficial persuasiveness. If one feels that one is helpless in the face of power which weighs on one like a great burden, then it is an easy step to say that all one's misfortunes, losses, unhappiness are attributable to the actions of an impenetrable, malevolent entity or institution that monopolises power and functions in a near superhuman fashion. It has to be near superhuman, otherwise one's supposed lack of agency would no longer be total and, heaven forfend, one might actually be able to engage with whatever it is that is weighing on one. Incompleteness thus gives birth to the polar opposite of agency – the sense of complete helplessness.

That, however, is intolerable, hence the explanation that one's own lack of power is balanced by someone else's accumulation of power. Once this zero-sum pattern of thinking has taken root, it is extremely difficult to shift, even to influence, because ideological thinking has an internal logic, albeit from a false premise, and proceeds to construct a thought-world or plausibility structure (Berger) that explains all, without anomalies or gaps or chance or accident. A further potential step in this chain is when the phenomenon acquires a group quality and is transformed into an enclave (Douglas). Enclaves surround themselves with a "wall of virtue" (attributed to oneself), which then protects the group from the vices of the outside world. This process becomes particularly dysfunctional when it affects a political group or party, which concludes that it is powerless, that others are illicitly exercising monopoly power and the sole defence (and hope for the future) is to denounce the wickedness of the outside world as loudly as possible, to shout Voltaire's *écrasez l'infâme*! That strengthens one's isolation and, crucially, acts as a defence against possible defection by reinforcing the group's identity. Extreme cases take a further step and, in effect, claim that because virtue is theirs, they cannot commit wrong and thereby set in motion a typical antinomian process (Hogg). Extremist movements of all colours are vulnerable to this process and it does not take much to initiate movement towards the extreme – polarisation is much more frequent when agency is felt to be lacking.

Another dimension of the lack of agency is Cassirer's mythic thinking (Friedman). The realworld, real–time present is found to be so intolerable that collective narratives come into being (are constructed); and these can then offer explanations for one's sense of marginalisation. These narratives are mythic because they are supraspatial and supratemporal, lived as immanent, are derived from a particular and particularistic reading of the past, are structured around a positive-negative polarity and may or may not offer salvation (religious, secular) as the terminal point. These polarities are linear, they offer hope (false, often enough) in a teleology that can acquire the qualities of an eschatology, possibly even the promise of rebirth (palingenesis, to stay with theological language), when finally all the wrongs suffered will be righted. All this is a long way from resembling Enlightenment rationality, though it can be seen as a perverted variant of the same, but then when the promise of the Enlightenment is not fulfilled, as it regularly isn't, an explanatory mechanism is vital. The thought that maybe the promise is itself flawed does not and cannot enter into the equation.

Czesław Miłosz (1983) noted that those from the periphery of Europe – and this applies potentially to the whole of Central Europe – are better placed to see Europe in the round than those who are at the centre. In fact, Miłosz was not in any sense relying on centre-periphery theory, would certainly have had little time for Wallerstein (at a guess) and, to some extent, even contradicted himself. In his poem "Bypassing rue Descartes", he explicitly denies that the world has a centre (he was obviously thinking of Paris), but for many in Western Europe, theirs remains the only true, authentic, possible way of thinking and acting. Hence, they have extreme difficulty in accepting that the Central European difference is not something malevolent or just contrarian, but is the outcome of longue durée historical processes to which they and their forebears contributed in no mean quantity. Don't even think about applying postcolonial theory to intra-European relations, might be their slogan. The result is an endless series of misperceptions and disappointments.

From the perspective of the Central Europeans, on the other hand, the West is often enough a resource of inspiration and dashed hopes. This is generally the case when we mythicise something that also has a real-world existence. The harsh reality is that the West, which of course does not and cannot exist as a single entity, has its own interests, agendas and identities and will, therefore, be guided by those and not by the wish-fulfilment fantasies of the Central Europeans. That's the trouble with mythlands, they seldom conform to the myth, as Stalin's and Mao's fellow travellers discovered. Not that that stopped the fellow-travelling, needless to say. It is the same with Central Europeans, or some of them anyway. They have high hopes of the West but end up being used by it.

One useful illustration of this process is the iconic Hungarian literary journal *Nyugat* (1908–1941). The word "nyugat" means West and the very title can be seen as a manifesto, that Hungarian culture and nation were and are a part of the West. The central difficulty with this claim, which for what it is worth, is seldom contested in Hungary, is that the West that was reflected in the pages of the journal was around 20 years out of date and was strongly orientated towards France, as a half-conscious response to the strong German influence on Hungary. This Francophilia was severely tested by the Treaty of Trianon, under the terms of which France gave away very large Hungarian-inhabited territories to its Czech, Romanian and Yugoslav clients. (To disclose a personal connection here, my grandfather, Aladár Schöpflin, was a leading figure in *Nyugat's* activities. I rather fear that he would have disapproved of what I have written.)

The difficulty is, that when seen from Central Europe, the West is necessarily homogenised and transformed into something that it isn't, an idealised and superior version of oneself – reality would be far too erosive. When Central Europeans think about the West, they seldom ask by what criteria are they defining it, what is the domestic context of their definition, why are they trying to define it at all? This is the perfect place to introduce (in brief) the double hermeneutic. This theory basically argues that there is an interactive relationship between observer and observed, that unlike inert matter, that which is observed has agency, while the observer has his or her cultural baggage, hence the much vaunted scientific objectivity of the positivists is nonsense. But so far, the theory has assumed a more or less equal relationship between observer and observed. In the case of the West and Central Europe, this is not accurate, because the former can generally ignore the latter, unless the latter makes a nuisance of herself (like engaging in a war or triggering one off). Hence what tends to happen is that the impact of the West on Central Europe is far more significant than the reverse, which then yet again reproduces the foresaid dynamic. Currently, the West still enjoys the privilege of superior cultural and moral power and exercises this mostly discursively (EU regulations are another matter). Local compradors then translate this Western discursivity, with its moral legislation (Bauman) into local conditions, where it encounters resistance and then the mechanism is set in motion yet again.

One final area in this fraught relationship is worth looking at and this takes us back to Kundera's insight that Central Europe functions as an early warning system for Europe. If we accept that incompleteness is the defining quality of Central Europe, then it is worth noting that something very similar is beginning to affect the West, as a consequence of globalisation. The well-established states of the West have begun to lose their discursive hegemony, are beginning to discover social segmentation (not least though the parallel societies that immigration has brought into being) and are, as a result, displaying familiar symptoms of insecurity and anxiety about their cultural reproduction (see France). That, in turn, is giving rise to the growing nationalism-rebranded-as-national-interest, which then makes the West resemble Central Europe – not of course that West Europeans would ever admit this, but then being ignored is generally the fate of the subaltern.

References

Babits, Mihály. 2008. *Légy ellenállás*. Budapest: Nap.

Bauman, Zygmunt. 1987. *Legislators and Interpreters* Cambridge: Polity.

Berger, Peter L. 1967. *The Sacred Canopy: Elements of a Sociological Theory of Religion*. New York: Doubleday.

Bibó, István. 1981. "A kelet-európai kisállamok nyomorúsága". In Bibó, István *Összegyűjtött munkái*, Vol.4, 202-251. Bern: Az Európai Protestáns Magyar Szabadegyetem.

Chmel, Rudolf. 2008. *Egy érzelmes (közép-) európai*. Bratislava: Kalligram.

Douglas, Mary. 1985. *Risk Acceptability according to the Social Sciences*. London: Routledge.

Fardon, Richard. 1999. *Mary Douglas: an Intellectual Biography*. London: Routledge.

Friedman, Michael. 2011. *Ernst Cassirer*. http://plato.stanford.edu/entries/cassirer/ downloaded 22 April 2011.

Garton Ash, Timothy. 1999. "The Puzzle of Central Europe". *New York Review of Books*. Vol.46, No.5, 18 March 1999.

Hogg, James. 1999. *The Private Memoirs and Confessions of a Justified Sinner*. Oxford: Oxford University Press.

Kopeček, Michal, *Politics, Antipolitics, and Czechs in Central Europe: The Idea of "Visegrád Cooperation" and Its Reflection in Czech Politics in the 1990s*. www.iwm.at/publ-jvc/jc-12-01.pdf downloaded 21 April 2011.

Kundera, Milan. 1984a. "The Tragedy of Central Europe", *New York Review of Books*, 26 April 1984 http://www.kx.hu/kepek/ises/anyagok/Kundera_tragedy_of_Central_Europe.pdf. The French version, "Un occident kidnappé", appeared in *Le Débat* in 1983/5 No.27.

Kundera, Milan. 1986. *The Art of the Novel*. Translated by Linda Asher. New York: Grove Press.

Kundera, Milan. 2007. *The Curtain: an Essay in Seven Parts*. Translated by Linda Asher London: Faber.

Kundera, Milan. 2009. *Találkozás*. Translated by Zsuzsa N. Kiss. Budapest: Európa.

Miłosz, Czesław. 1983. *The Witness of Poetry*. Cambridge MA: Harvard University Press.

Miłosz, Czesław. 2001. *Proud to be a Mammal: Essays on War, Faith and Memory*. London: Penguin.

Peiker, Piret. 2004. "Legitimacy and Fluidity: Central European Narratives of Personhood", *Acta Collegii Humaniorum Estoniensis*, 220-238

Péteri, György. "Imagining the West – Perceptions of the Western Other in Modern and Contemporary Eastern Europe and Turkey", www.hf.ntnu.no/peecs/home/images/stories/PDF_filer/imagining_web.pdf. Downloaded 5 April 2011.

Schöpflin, George and Nancy Wood, eds. 1989. *In Search of Central Europe*. Cambridge: Polity.

Schöpflin, George. 2000. *Nations, Identity, Power: the New Politics of Europe*. London: Hurst.

Schöpflin, George. 2010. *The Dilemmas of Identity*. Tallinn: Tallinn University Press.

Shakespeare, William. *Romeo and Juliet*, Act II, scene ii, lines 1-2. The quotation in full: Juliet: "What's in a name? That which we call a rose By any other name would smell as sweet."

Verdery, Katherine. 1983. *Transylvanian Villagers: Three Centuries of Political, Economic, and Ethnic Change*. Berkeley: University of California Press.

Liberalism, Human Rights, Populism*

There is a major tension at the heart of the European project, the tension between human rights and conflict resolution. That conflict resolution was the founding principle of European integration is incontestable, but currently that principle is increasingly marginalised in favour of human rights. The two are not the same and, while not necessarily incompatible, they prioritise different outcomes, different processes, have different consequences and affect different fields of political power, whether at the EU level or that of the member state.

The implication of this argument is that when it comes to European politics, we should shift our focus away from "populism", "illiberal democracy", "xenophobia", "nativism" and other sins, because these are the surface phenomena of a much deeper conflict. And until these depths are explored and clarified, the crisis in European politics will persist and, quite likely, intensify.

Basically both human rights and conflict resolution are based on a moral imperative – the former on a particular reading of the equality of identities, the latter on securing the consensual handling of contests of power. Both equality and consent have a moral content, even while they can be and are translated into practical action which then obscures the moral starting point. Where the two principles do diverge is in their openness to political contest.

---

* Published online at http://schopflingyorgy.hu/en/liberalism-human-rights-populism.

Conflict resolution is explicitly political and calls upon the parties involved to resolve their differences through the debate and compromise that is the heart of democracy. Human rights, on the other hand, claims to transcend politics and demands that all political action be subordinated to its moral principles. In this sense, human rights is making a truth-claim that there are values – conceivably a single value – that must normatively structure democracy. It follows, and this has grave consequences, that basing a political system on human rights makes democratic self-limitation and compromise considerably more difficult to achieve.

One way of addressing this problem of a superordinate system of moral values is to use the framework delineated by Isaiah Berlin in his *New York Review* essay. In this essay, Berlin argued strongly for value pluralism and against the dangers of moral monism. Crucially, he makes the point that some values are incommensurable:

> What is clear is that values can clash—that is why civilizations are incompatible. They can be incompatible between cultures, or groups in the same culture, or between you and me. You believe in always telling the truth, no matter what; I do not, because I believe that it can sometimes be too painful and too destructive. We can discuss each other's point of view, we can try to reach common ground, but in the end what you pursue may not be reconcilable with the ends to which I find that I have dedicated my life. Values may easily clash within the breast of a single individual; and it does not follow that, if they do, some must be true and others false. Justice, rigorous justice, is for some people an absolute value, but it is not compatible with what may be no less ultimate values for them—mercy, compassion, as arises in concrete cases.

The trouble with the human rights discursivity is that it rejects this, that it claims that human transactions (all? most?) can be, should be assessed by human rights criteria. Note here that the human rights discursivity is dynamic, potentially protean, applicable universally and not susceptible to challenge. In this, it has come to resemble a faith-based system of norms, rather than a rational, presumably falsifiable, postulate. Certainly, human rights has become strongly sacralised, meaning that it is above questioning; indeed those who do question it, its universal applicability, are open to ever stronger condemnation.

If we look at the evolution of the rights discourse, its contingency immediately becomes evident and once the contingency is clear, it can be seen for what it has become, a particular facet of Western intellectual thought with deep historical roots, but importantly only one among many. Here is John Gray's insight:

> The overriding importance given to rights – a selective reading of them, at any rate – is one of the marks of the new liberalism. In one form or another, doctrines of human rights have been around for centuries, and a conception of universal rights was embodied in the UN Declaration of 1948. But rights became central and primary in liberal thought only in the 1970s with the rise of the legalist philosophies of John Rawls and Ronald Dworkin, which held that freedom can be codified into a fixed system of interlocking liberties that can be interpreted by judges. On the libertarian right, Friedrich Hayek proposed something similar with his constitutional proposals for limiting democracy.

Liberal values are, then, self-evidently not universal, but are projected as such normatively; in sociological reality, they are the preserve of particular sections of society, above all, sections of the elite. By the same token, these values are rooted in the particular world of Europe and North America and, therefore, clash with the local value systems in non-Europe. This does not in any way necessarily make them base or evil, but in common with all human endeavour, liberalism is contingent and open to interrogation. Yet there can evolve a particular cognitive situation when a set of values becomes the hegemonic, self-legitimating ideology of a particular stratum of society which then essentialises the ideology, transforms it into a facet of its identity and insists on its universality. And that it is axiomatic. This is the current problematic.

In such processes, whatever the value system that we are assessing, they acquire a strong tendency to become inward-looking and reluctant to change. Worse, its protagonists will seldom or never engage with alternatives, critiques, questioning, but will dismiss these as hostile. Note that this sketch was equally true of other closed systems, like Marxism-Leninism, Fascism (the real one), Freudianism, some variants of Christianity, fundamentalist Islam to name a but a few. Unfortunately this essentialisation has also captured and captivated some of the representatives of contemporary liberalism. The principles elaborated by Mill and Tocqueville have been transformed into something more closed and inward looking, turned into a self-legitimating ideology with boundaries, a metalanguage and metaphors – it bears an eerie resemblance to other identity collectives.

Note here the growing intensity, the emotionality, of the metalanguage preferred by human rights protagonists, none of which points towards the necessary understanding of the other's perspective. If anything, the language in question is prima facie negative, dismissive and condemnatory, more and more excluding respect for one's political opponents. Indeed, the distinction between opponent and enemy is fading (this works even better in Hungarian, "ellenzék" and "ellenség" are etymologically linked, but wholly distinct in meaning). To describe one's political opponents as "populists" etc. comes close to denying their moral worth as human beings, let alone accepting them as citizens. The dangers of this radical disavowal should be clear to all, yet – or so I see in far too many places – it is widespread and increasingly so, whether among politicians, think tanks, civil society or the media.

"Populism" is in itself a concept that is all but impossible to define coherently, other than as the binary opposite of whatever the liberal value system decrees at a particular moment. Still, here is one attempt to do so by someone with impeccable liberal credentials, Jan-Werner Müller: "Rather, populists claim that they and they alone speak in the name of what they tend to call the 'real people' or the 'silent majority'."

What this definition does not do, however, is to take the process further and ask who are the individuals who make up the mythic people. It is here that we find paradox and contradiction. The "people" are not on-ly the putative whole imagined (in Anderson's sense) by politicians, but are at the same time, citizens, voters, society, public opinion, the pub-lic sphere, the nation in certain contexts. In the international context, it is a people that have the right to self-determination. The people are also those with the right to exercise popular sovereignty.

What Müller's definition further fails to do is to ask the question "why?" Why are people listening to populists, what is missing from the message of mainstream liberalism? What effect does it have when the mainstream's message is that the populists are "bad people"? What is there in this message that impels people to vote for populism?

Basically, the only logical response is that as the "people" voters cease to be citizens or are bad citizens, because in the liberal world-view a cit-izen must be a liberal and accept that liberals know best. So, the people had better be deprived of their agency, such as voting, if they don't follow the precepts of the liberal elite. To anyone with a sense of history this is beginning to resemble a vanguard party as Lenin constructed it. At least there are no Gulags yet, though the functional equivalent of the show trial can be found in the social media.

The argument in favour of a distinctively less moralised approach to political action, whether at the European or the member state level, de-rives from the founding principles of European integration – conflict resolution – which in themselves are at the core of democratic theory. In sum, there will always be conflict, disagreement, disapproval, hence these cannot be expelled from human societies other than by suppres-sion and violence.

If we begin from the proposition that suppression and violence must be excluded, we have to establish other ways to resolving conflict. It was here that the European integration process required a remarkable act of innovation, to argue that the bargaining, dealing, compromise char-acteristic of democracy could be raised to the higher, inter-state level if states were prepared to surrender some of their sovereignty to a supra-state institution.

That much is commonplace, as are the problems of remoteness, democratic accountability, technocratic inflexibility and the other ills associated with the European Union. What should be clear from the foregoing is that the problems listed here will not be resolved by an exclusive or hegemonic reliance on human rights. Crucially, this arises from their divergent bases in what to do with values in conflict. Following Isaiah Berlin, we can argue that democratic compromise accepts the incommensurability of certain values (justice and compassion are ones he notes) and seeks to establish an equilibrium between competing values.

Yet the transcendental moral superiority attributed to human rights points rather towards moral monism. I do not wish to be misunderstood here. The champions of human rights do not have access to Gulag or concentration camps, but their monism makes them potentially and structurally – repeat, structurally – similar to the great totalitarian systems of Twentieth Century Europe. So, to exaggerate a bit, what we are looking at is a kind of High Authority on human rights which has begun to resemble a postmodern inquisition in its methodology.

This definition of the Frankfurt School remains relevant to the liberal elite:

> The one trait that the savants of the Frankfurt School shared with Hollywood executives was a fundamental tendency to underestimate, even to hold in contempt, the common man, despite the fact that the common man was the very focus of their attention and efforts. (Banville).

To bring this argument to a more concrete level, the proliferation of human rights instruments should be as much subject to sceptical scrutiny as any other initiative. Second, if there is to be a single standard for human rights in the EU, one that is fully legitimate, it must apply evenhandedly to all member states and must remain within the realm of law. Third, the moment that human rights is touched by either leftwing or rightwing interests, it loses its legitimacy as a legally neutral process.

As far as the even-handedness is concerned, whether this was intentional or not, too much attention has been afforded to actions against Poland and Hungary. Is everyone truly satisfied that these are the only two member states where one might identify "systemic risks" to the rule of law? One can discern a "narrative of democratic backsliding" applied to Central Europe that is not applied elsewhere in the EU. This then serves to reinforce a kind of ongoing post-enlargement process that questions the full and equal EU membership that these states were promised on accession.

Hence for the EU to recover its legitimacy and élan, there will have to be a far-reaching reappraisal of what the elites are doing, why their solutions fail to resonate, where the dividing line between law and politics should be drawn and defended and, maybe above all, to avoid the temptations of power and moral legislation. This last has deep roots in Europe and may well be the hardest to abandon. Zygmunt Bauman's assessment has not lost its validity. But if the liberal elites fail in this, other elites will transcend them. Indeed, this process is already happening.

Looked at from the bottom up, a sizeable section of society (citizens, voters, the people) has concluded that the dominant elites no longer represent their view of the world, resulting in a loss of cultural legitimacy. Hence, the moral order constructed by the liberal elite is not that of much of society. This has political consequences, most obviously in the outcomes of elections – in 2016 alone, these elites have been rejected in the Netherlands, the United Kingdom, in the USA and in Italy; in the Austrian presidential elections, the liberal elite managed to defeat the anti-establishment challenger. From the liberal perspective, this ought to be seen as a serious warning, but to date the response has been to double up, to insist that liberalism is always right. As ever, the Platonic ideal of elite rule is never far away.

To conclude, let us assume that 2016 is a hinge year in the history of the West and of the democratic order. The observable change is that the liberal hegemony has received a series of body blows, but continues to resist the conclusion that liberalism – in its current articulation – is unsustainable in a democratic environment where the electorate can express views at variance with the assumption set of the hegemony. The liberal project has failed. The assimilation of the great majority of society to liberal values has not taken place, even if the liberal elites refuse to recognise this. For sizeable swathes of society, while some liberal values may be accepted, neither the package as a whole nor the application of these values have been. Whereas liberals have spent a great deal of time on the equality of various minority groups, they have neglected the core white majority and the majority doesn't like it. The neglect has obviously been economic, but far more important has been status and moral equality. The moral legislation pursued by the elite necessarily casts the majority into an inferior position.

If we interpret the liberal-populist tension as a positive-negative polarity, then we can see two things. First, by placing liberalism at the end of a polarity, its contingency becomes visible, so that its protagonists can no longer proclaim it as normal and natural. It is one set of moral claims among many others. The emergence of this polarity has, thus, helped to erode the "exemplary and binding" quality that liberalism proclaimed. Second, assuming that democratic conditions will hold, over time the liberal elite will gradually become weaker than society, given that the latter no longer accepts elite guidance so readily and, equally, has elevated counter-elites that express a divergent (non-liberal) view of the world.

The obvious implication is that there is no guarantee that any hegemony will remain in business forever and that the protagonists of liberalism have yet to confront the realisation that their reign is not eternal. There is no end of history, in other words. Many continue to think otherwise. A further implication of this argument is that linear views of history are mistaken and that history does not have sides, hence there is no "progress", no historical inevitability either.

The liberal thought-world does not differ from other analogous phenomena. It is constructed and works as long as it resonates. What cannot be seen at this time is what results the polarity with populism will have. Some of those inside the thought-world will be invigorated by the struggle, even when external realities are ever more remote the liberal norms. But a parallel scenario is also possible. Liberalism will evolve into a meta-language, but its content will erode, until some new discourse will take its place. This was more or less the fate of Marxism-Leninism. No parallel is exact, of course.

The rising populist elites face a different set of dilemmas. If they are to gain power, they will have to deradicalise and find a connection to the centre; this raises the danger of losing the radical base, but without making serious inroads in the middle ground. And then, once in power, they have to demonstrate that their policies work, that they deliver on their promises and that they do actually improve things in the eyes of the support base. Otherwise, their followers will desert them.

So, what next? If liberalism does want to remain in business, and liberal values are a necessary condition of democracy, then it must shed its increasingly closed categories and rethink what it regards as genuinely important for a democratic order. Equality – maybe equivalence is preferable – of status and mutual respect must be at the top of the list. Then, there must be a recognition of the proposition that collective identities do matter, and this includes all collective identities, not merely those that the liberals have chosen to privilege. Nationhood is very much among them.

Similarly, majorities do have rights, so that occasionally – as the outcome of debate – minorities have to give way to majorities, though not all the way, as this is and must be a case of ongoing negotiation. Then, there is the question of values. It should be evident that some values are negative and, following Isaiah Berlin, some are incommensurable. It is not enough to declaim values, they must be specified and argued.

Debate has declined. The liberal hegemony has acquired the bad habit of ignoring arguments that it does not like or cannot answer, and that includes empirical data. If liberal values are to survive and not be swamped by negatives, they must be part of a contest, which is something that liberals have forgotten, seemingly. Furthermore, it would be helpful if liberalism reconnected with its 19th-century roots and abandoned its claim to the omniscience that it has taken over from Marxism-Leninism. Notably, liberalism appears to have accepted a variant of false consciousness from which the people are suffering. This notion really should end up in the dustbin of history.

The legacy of vulgarised Foucault, that all power is dubious, is similarly suspect – the legacy cannot be applied to all situations, above all state power offers predictability, security and order. Thus the state is not invariably, inherently undesirable; NGOs please pay attention.

Ultimately, if democracy is to live as a system that applies to all, then liberalism must pay heed to particularism, to local traditions and expectations. The one-size-fits-all universalism is, therefore, a threat to liberalism itself, because it empowers precisely the very authoritarians that liberalism would like to eliminate. And that scenario would be the worst irony of them all.

The seeming polyphony of globalisation has defaulted into a binary opposition, as is so often the case. The two polarities – liberalism and populism – are to an extent misnomers. Liberalism is not very liberal and who can say what populism really is? Third, populism in its present form has been constructed by the liberal opposition to it, it has been the liberal attributions by which this populism is defined. Another facet of this is that the binary opposition has given new strength to a much older one, the one between universalism and particularism. After about two decades of ruling the roost, the discourse of universalism has found a challenger. Finally, precisely by defining populism through a series of negative attributions, liberalism has ensured that it has a role in the democratic system, an undesirable one for some, but still better inside it than outside.

January 2017

References

Anderson, Benedict. 2006. *Imagined Communities: Reflections on the Origin and Spread of Nationalism*. Verso.

Banville. John. 2016. "The View from the Tower", *Dublin Review of Books*, December. http://www.drb.ie/essays/the-view-from-the-tower

Bauman, Zygmunt. 1987. , *Legislators and Interpreters: On modernity, post-modernity and intellectuals*. Polity.

Berlin, Isaiah. 1988. "On the Pursuit of the Ideal", *New York Review of Books*, 17 March. http://faculty.up.edu/asarnow/351/Berlin%20Pursuit%20of%20the%20 Ideal.htm

Furedi, Frank. 2016. "Populism: a defence", *Spiked*. November. http://www. spiked-online.com/spiked-review/article/populism-a-defence/19042?utm_ content=bufferee163&utm_medium=social&utm_source=twitter.com&utm_ campaign=buffer#.WENBEpJSIUV

Gray, John. 2016. "The closing of the liberal mind", *New Statesman*. 8 November. http:// www.newstatesman.com/politics/uk/2016/11/closing-liberal-mind?utm_source= New+Daily+Newsletter+Subscribers&u tm_campaign=691e1f9d96- EMAIL_ CAMPAIGN_2016_11_08&utm_medium=email &utm_term=0_4675a5c15f-691e1f9d96-81848629

Werner-Müller, Jan. 2016. "Capitalism in One Family", *London Review of Books*. 1 December. http://www.lrb.co.uk/v38/n23/jan-werner-muller/capitalism-in-one-family

Political lessons for Central Europe
from Orbán's Hungary*

There are several ways of interpreting the patterns of Hungarian politics since 2010 and they are wildly contradictory. On the part of the Western and local left, there is thoroughgoing rejection, as much a moral as a political statement. Whatever Viktor Orbán's government does, on this view, is inherently abhorrent. For those who espouse this view, it is a naturalised fact – "fact" would be more correct – that the political system in Hungary has become, is becoming or is moving towards authoritarianism. The Hungarian left consistently uses the word "regime" to characterise the Orbán government in the full knowledge that, in the currently accepted political vocabulary, the word regime usually applies to dictatorships. For some, Hungary is simply inexplicable, at best something like a consensual semi-democratic system. To my knowledge, no one has as yet claimed that the Fidesz government was not elected democratically and that it will not cede power if it should be defeated, but that appears to make no difference. Then there are those for whom Hungary and what goes on there are inexplicable and, hence, not worth bothering with.

Despite the flood of negative criticism from virtually all the Western media, the most recent period has seen the beginnings of a more positive evaluation of Orbán and Fidesz. This is overwhelmingly tied up with

* Published originally in *Aspen Review* No.2, 2016. http://www.aspeninstitute.cz/en/article/2-2016-political-lessons-for-central-europe-from-orban-s-hungary.

the migration crisis, but a part of it can be attributed to the position that Hungary has adopted towards the EU Commission, a stance that strongly stresses member state sovereignty and is very hostile to the enlargement of EU powers "by stealth" – *lopakodó* is the Hungarian word and it incorporates the concept of "stealing" much as the English does. Actually, this push to enlarge powers is overt and in the public sphere, but is hardly ever understood by the media, hence such moves arrive abruptly. A case in point is the Rule of Law Framework activated by the Commission against Poland in January 2016; it had, in fact, been on the books since March 2014, but had remained buried in obscurity because the Brussels media failed to notice it.

The positive evaluation of Orbán mentioned above, where he can be considered a trail-blazer, though probably not a role-model can be assessed through an analysis of five areas – migration, the relationship between the EU and the member states, "illiberalism", the position of the Visegrád states and leadership.

First, however, I want to offer an analysis of the broad context within which the Fidesz government has been operating and this requires a few words on how the criteria of evaluation come into being. Basically, this is a question of the legitimation of knowledge, what information is deemed acceptable (and by whom), how political judgements are formed, what assertions are converted into accepted, naturalised facts.

What should have emerged from the foregoing is that the gap between representation and reality of Hungary is substantial and growing. This deserves a short assessment. The liberal consensus that emerged after the collapse of communism, with the so-called end of history, rapidly captured the post-Marxist elites, so that by 2010, when Fidesz gained a two-thirds majority, these elites implicitly saw themselves as the vanguard of history and understood their role as hegemonic. A cogent piece of supporting evidence is the equally rapid spread of the expression "the wrong side of history". A moment's thought will demonstrate that this is no more than a spatial metaphor, that history does not have sides, for if it did, would it not also have a top and a bottom, an inside and an outside? But the phrase was and is useful to legitimate the superior – morally, politically, economically – values of liberalism against all challengers.

It is at this point that Foucault's power/knowledge equation became applicable to the liberal elite, even while (ironically) a part of their worldview, the deep suspicion of the state and state power was inherited more from Foucault than anyone else. In short, what the liberal elites arrogated to themselves was the hegemony of the production of knowledge and its legitimation. I used the words "vanguard" and "implicit" in the above. Both, I would suggest, are applicable. The members of the elite consensus are remarkably intolerant of challengers, whether from the left or the right, precisely because of the self-attributed vanguard quality and implicit because it is preferable to keep it opaque rather than transparent, for that way it remains difficult to challenge (as I am doing). Obviously this is not a vanguard in the strict Leninist sense; it is satisfied with hegemony and is not, to the best of my knowledge, planning to establish Gulag.

A further irony is that the consensus places transparency well in the foreground of their values – virtues – but will seldom apply it to its own axiology. The standard technique is to ignore critiques and if that fails, to denounce them as populist, xenophobic or just coming from the wrong side of history. And being the vanguard of history further means that one does not have to bother with one's own contingency, which then impacts on the values, rights, aspirations of those outside the consensus – they're on the wrong side, so there.

It is worth noting here that the hegemony of the liberal consensus is beginning to be questioned by parts of left. Austerity, inequality, stagnation can be seen as the triggers. And there are some signs that a section of the socialist left is coming to question its absorption by liberalism and is looking for a path that confronts inequality, community, and responsibility (Streeck).

This was the background against which the success of Fidesz has to be understood. How was it possible for a centre-right party to gain a two-thirds majority, when it was self-evidently on the wrong side of you-know-what? So, denounce it. The *Süddeutsche Zeitung* did just that, even before the Fidesz government published its programme. And the attacks have continued and do so to this day. This negative climate has obviously influenced Fidesz and Orbán himself. On the face of it, it is possible to argue that Fidesz had the choice to back-pedal or tread water, but the situation in Hungary was so dire after the disastrous left-liberal governments of 2002–2010, that urgent action was essential. Worse, the policies of these governments were unquestionably liberal, so that a radical, non-liberal alternative was the only feasible strategy. This was what the Fidesz government pursued.

Migrants

If one were to try and identify a turning point in the assessments of the Fidesz government, both at home and abroad, this was unquestionably the 2015 migration crisis. Hungary lies athwart the south-north migrant route to Germany and, abetted by human smugglers, around 400,000 persons (of varied backgrounds) marched through Hungary as if it were not there, as if this was a non-country, just an empty territory. Hungary has obligations under the EU's Dublin regulations to register everyone crossing a Schengen frontier, which Hungary's southern border with Serbia is, and to protect that border against breaches. The migrants paid no attention to this whatever. The presence of the migrants – technically illegal immigrants unless they registered – was amplified by the none-too-Fidesz-friendly Western and Hungarian opposition media, notably in showing pictures almost exclusively of women and children, even while three-quarters of the migrants were young adult males. This was recognised as manipulation on an industrial scale. The government had to act and chose to build a fence along the frontier – the foresaid media invariably described it as a "razor-wire" fence, to communicate its fearful quality. The construction of the fence brought a torrent of criticism, from Western politicians, as well as media. The Hungarian answer was and is, Dublin and Schengen, do you have an alternative? The reluctant acknowledgement was "no", but we still don't like the fence. So damned if you do, damned if you don't. Not surprisingly, complaints of double standards began to fill the air.

As it turned out, it was one thing to be generally in favour of the migrants, as much of Western opinion seemed to be, and something else to be dealing with real, live migrants. Angela Merkel's *Willkommenskultur* was well received at first, but this welcome started fraying at the edges under both the immense strain that the arrivals were placing on the German administration and public services, as well as the behaviour of (some of) the migrants themselves. At this point, the tension between liberal individualism and collective representation became acute – a few negative cases were enough to raise questions over all migrants and especially Muslims. The collective representation issue also applied to Hungary, of course. Was the government representative of all Hungarians? This was not a distinction that many stopped to make.

While Western opinion formers were generally uneasy to hostile regarding the Fidesz government, in the Visegrád countries Orbán's stance was well received. Indeed, the Slovak prime minister Robert Fico went out of his way to praise Hungary, which is quite extraordinary to anyone who knows how sensitive these relations have been. The Polish and Czech governments were likewise content with the role that Hungary was playing. Note that this is a very old historical topos shared by all the national mythopoeias of Central Europe, that they constitute the bastion of Europe against the invaders from the east. There is some historical truth in this.

In the contexts of the migrants, there were several further turning points. The slaughter of 130 people in Paris in November 2015 undergirded the proposition that some of the migrants were terrorists, something that the liberal consensus systematically denied. Much of public opinion concluded otherwise. Orbán's position on this was that those arriving fell into three separate categories – asylum seekers, economic migrants and fighters. This categorisation was not widely accepted, understandably from the perspective of the consensus as it was a form of knowledge production that went against the hegemony. But the New Year's Eve clashes in Cologne can be seen as a sea-change, above all because it clearly showed the attitude of some Muslims towards women; matters were made worse by the cover-up by the local authorities. There was an underswell of anger in Germany that heavily eroded the *Willkommenskultur* and once or twice there were certainly demonstrators carrying pro-Orbán placards.

Orbán basically represented the polar opposite of *Willkommenskultur*, so that the range of opinion on migration stretched from Orbán to Merkel. This was in itself significant, because Orbán was inside the tent, in the European People's Party (unlike Marine le Pen or Geert Wilders), so that he offered an acceptable alternative to Merkel's "let's have everyone come to Germany" policy. It is worth adding here, possibly essential to add here, that for all practical purposes Merkel imposed a policy on the EU, without consultation, so that Orbán's "no" to uncontrolled migration was a clear, incontrovertible alternative.

This did not make him universally popular. There were repeated demands from the centre-left voices for the EPP to expel Fidesz. Evidently they recognised that Orbán's alternative was a dangerous one – dangerous because it resonated with sections of public opinion, because it was a frontal challenge to the hegemony of the left and because it represented a conflicting moral value, that of the right to choose something other than that approved by the consensus.

The EU

Fidesz did not start out as an anti-EU party and it still isn't, albeit it has strong reservations about some of the policies of the EU. In many respects, it is the EU that has changed, accepting and adopting many of the assumptions of the liberal consensus. In this sense, the agenda of European integration has been captured in such a way as to exclude some (not all) of conservative and Christian Democrat thinking. The discourses of human rights, rule of law or checks-and-balances have weakened state sovereignty and the market-liberal assumptions of the Commission had an equivocal effect on the economies of the former communist member states.

The first Orbán government (1998–2002) negotiated much of the accession agreement and was committed to membership. Some doubts set in when, with Fidesz in opposition, the Commission passed lightly over the excessive deficits of the left-liberal governments and looked the other way when the demonstration on the 50th anniversary of the 1956 revolution was dispersed with brutality by the then government. There was a general sense that leftwing governments were treated much more gently than rightwing ones.

In 2010, after winning the election, Fidesz discovered that the economic and financial situation was considerably worse than it had understood – more creative accounting by the left – and asked the Commission for an easing of terms, of the 3 percent limit. This was rejected. Austerity was the order of the day, forcing the government to cut back and, at the same time, impelling it to recover its independence through growth. As Orbán repeated more than once, Hungary nearly went the way of Greece and would thereby have lost its sovereignty. This rejection was, I rather believe, a shock to Fidesz as unexpected and was inexplicable other than as a double standard, in as much as the pre-2010 governments were let off much more lightly.

The conflict with the Commission continued and here we have the evidence of Helga Wiedermann to rely on. As head of the economic minister's cabinet, she saw the conflict from a close perspective. Wiedermann argues that the financial commissioner, Olli Rehn, a Finnish liberal, sought to impose an austerity policy on Hungary, which the government was entirely unprepared to accept. Instead of restrictions, the government planned to impose taxes on banks, telecoms and other large-scale enterprises (usually foreign owned). This was heresy and set a very bad example from the viewpoint of those affected and had to be stopped; "stopping" would include the toppling of the Fidesz government. The Commission appeared to be ready to go along with this. There were major battles at Ecofin meetings, which did finally allow Hungary to go its own way, including ending excessive deficit procedure.

But Ecofin was not the only battle ground. The Western media and the left in the European Parliament opened another front, with evident help from the Hungarian opposition. Predictably the media focused on the Hungarian Media Law which they presented as the de facto introduction of censorship. In reality, the Media Law was based on the practice of various other EU countries, but the attacks ignored this and sketched a picture of extreme restrictiveness. Interestingly, there was never any attempt to follow up what effect the Media Law actually had on the freedom of expression. It was simply taken for granted that matters were dreadful. The Commission, for its part, repeatedly scrutinised Hungarian legislation, on the media and other issues, and generally found that there were no major infractions. Problems were mostly sorted out through infringement procedures and dialogue, much to the detestation of the left.

The European Parliament as battle ground had two dimensions. There were repeated hearings about Hungary (I took part in six or seven of these representing the Fidesz MEPs) and what I still find fascinating is that counter-arguments were ignored. Habermas was proved wrong, sometimes you can't achieve much through rational discourse. But then you can't really argue with a hegemony. The other dimension, to simplify the story somewhat, was the contest over human rights and rule of law in the civil liberties committee (LIBE). This culminated in the report presented by the leftwing Portuguese MEP, Rui Tavares, which catalogued all sorts of major and minor malfeasance by the Fidesz government. At the same time, the utter unwillingness of the left to listen and discuss matters rationally was brought home to Hungarian viewers many of whom watched the plenary debates on webstream. This had the unintended consequence of delegitimating the European Parliament as far as centre-right opinion in Hungary was concerned.

Against this background, it is hardly surprising that relations with the EU – and only insiders make the distinction among Commission, Council and Parliament – should have become deeply envenomed. Hungary has repeatedly insisted on the primacy of state sovereignty, unless powers have been transferred, and is a strong supporter of intergovernmentalism. Attempts have been made to paint Hungary into the Eurosceptic corner, but this is inaccurate. Hungary will not leave the EU, but wants to see an EU that is more responsive to the aspirations of the people of Europe rather than to the left-federalism of EU insiders.

"Illiberalism"

It's hard to think of another word that resonated so strongly and so negatively as illiberalism, the word used by Orbán in his speech to the summer university at Tusnádfürdő/Băile Tuşnad in Transylvania (26 July 2014). Given the notoriety of the speech, it's worth looking at both the text and the context of what Orbán said. Here are some of the key passages:

> a race [is] underway to find the method of community organisation, the state, which is most capable of making a nation and a community internationally competitive

> [There is no necessary connection between a liberal state and economic success] "The stars of the international analysts today are Singapore, China, India, Russia and Turkey."

> [what we are] trying [is] to find the form of community organisation, the new Hungarian state, which is capable of making our community competitive in the great global race" [and] "**in this sense** the new state that we are constructing in Hungary is an illiberal state, a non-liberal state. It does not reject the fundamental principles of liberalism such as freedom [emphasis added]

It should be evident enough to anyone prepared to make the effort that the context of "illiberal" was specific to economics and, to some extent, ethics. Two things are crystal clear. Illiberalism does not mean the elimination of fundamental, democratic rights. And the mention of the economic success of the authoritarian states listed does not mean that they are exemplars to be followed – no, they are there to illustrate the thesis that liberalism is not a necessary condition of economic success, something very different.

But it's probably too much to expect liberal commentators to take the trouble with complex (well, not that complex) textual analysis and, hence, to offer a balanced account of Orbán's speech. From one perspective this is understandable, that of symbolics. To anyone inside the liberal mindset, the thought that the prime minister of a democratic state could actually mention word illiberal, let alone say that this was the method he was following, was worse than anathema, it was an abomination. In this regard, the reaction to illiberal was emotional, not rational, near hysterical and amidst the noise, it became impossible to discuss it *sine ira et studio*.

What the debate might have focused on is whether liberalism and democracy are eternally yoked, in other words, can there be non-liberal democracy? (Ober) Christian Democracy, Social Democracy, Conservativism have all existed, but have they been dispersed by liberal democracy? Has there been a quiet Hegelian sublation? Understandably those in the consensus just do not want to go there and ask questions about democracy and liberalism. And it's worth adding that there are those in the EPP who accept the hegemony of liberalism over democracy. No wonder, then, that Orbán's use of "illiberalism" caused such overreaction. It threatened every holy cow in sight and beyond.

The V4

We can set to one side the debate (in which I too have participated) as to whether there is such a thing as Central Europe. The Visegrád states recognised a certain set of shared interests and have constructed a fairly loose set of institutions to represent them. The V4 meet regularly at various levels, their governments coordinate positions at times regarding the EU, they have summits, a presidency and even a fund. All the same until the migration crisis, the V4 was never a very intense form of coordination. It was and is intergovernmental and basically does what its leaders are ready to accept, a kind of lowest common denominator. Some of the cooperation depends on there being like-minded governments in power and, indeed, to personal relations, giving V4 activities a certain contingent quality. The migration crisis, however, has found a notably high level agreement among the four leaderships and their public opinions – they don't want migrants, above all they do not want the Commission to be able to impose compulsory quotas, however low. It is the compulsory element to which they are opposed.

This common position has various elements. Self-evidently, V4 opinion formers have looked at the success/failure of integrating third world migrants, especially Muslims in the West, and have concluded that they want no part of it. Actually, all four countries have very small Muslim communities, but these are marginal to the argument. The hard reality is that Muslim migrant communities do not integrate well, that they have become the source of home-grown jihadi terrorism and that even when members of a community are well integrated, their loyalty will often be to the community rather than to the state of which they are citizens, meaning that they could well act as a safe haven to terrorists. The overall popular attitude in the V4 is that it does not want migrants, full stop. In parentheses, it is also true that very few migrants want Central Europe, they want to get to an idealised Germany or Sweden.

The argument from values is straightforward. If a country wishes to receive migrants and to be multicultural, that's fine. But by exactly the same token, if a country does not want to be multicultural, that should be assessed in the same fashion. Then, there is the argument from history. The 45 years of communism have marked these countries deeply; they felt that they were written off by the West – we can all recite Yalta, 1956, 1968, 1980 – and, hence that the West owes Central Europe, if nothing else, parity of esteem. I myself would add another argument from history, one that is seldom recognised. All the states of the region were part of at least one empire and are in that sense post-colonial, but the West has never accepted this proposition. Equally, Central Europeans have no post-colonial guilt and are, therefore, much less sympathetic to the mess made by colonial empires (e.g., Sykes-Picot). A third argument is from economics. These are significantly poorer countries than those of the West, so receiving migrants would be an added burden. A fourth argument turns round the Western attacks on some of the Central European states over human rights, notably the situation of the Roma. If human rights in these states are in such terrible condition, why does the West want send migrants there?

All these and other points have become fused into a single stance of resistance, symbolised by Orbán. He is seen as standing up for Hungary and thereby for Central Europe as a whole. The other V4 leaders have broadly endorsed this, with greater or lesser enthusiasm. Hungary joined Slovakia in appealing against the compulsory quota to the European Court of Justice. Together with Czech Republic they voted against the quota at the interior ministers' meeting (Poland voted to accept, but that decision was that of the previous government). I'm not suggesting that all this was the single-handed achievement of Orbán, but his strong stance has given the V4 an issue around which they can cohere, despite differences over Russia, say.

Leadership

It is always hard to see political figures in perspective. President de Gaulle was widely excoriated in his lifetime, but these days he is greatly admired (Fenby). In the same sense, it is both difficult and premature to offer an assessment of Orbán's role as leader. It is clear enough to anyone who has listened to him (as I have) that he is a compelling public speaker, that he has charisma and that he has the political courage to raise issues that most others leave well alone (e.g., "illiberalism"), even if some would call it foolhardy. He has also shown political skill in recognising that the migration issue was a major opportunity structure that affected the whole of Europe and that he himself could play a Europe-wide role by adopting it in the forthright fashion that he has.

To this should be added, in the context of leadership, his formulation and use of the phrase "ballot box revolution". By gaining a two-thirds majority, the road was open to launch a major transformation of Hungarian politics. The nomenklatura inherited from the communist period had found a new lease of life under the leftwing governments and its style of rule was decidedly top down. Orbán swept this away, starting with the new constitution, the Basic Law, and instituting reforms in virtually all areas of public life. He further brought in a different discursive system with emphasis on nationhood (including the ethnic Hungarian communities in the neighbouring states), the family, tradition and giving the symbolic Brussels an undeniably negative value. "Illiberalism" fits nicely into this discursive system. Arguably in broad historical terms Orbán's project was to relaunch an authentically Hungarian form of modernity, one that was broken by the collapse of historic Hungary after 1918. This project, especially once its boldness became evident, attracted widespread condemnation in the West, but resonated with much of Hungarian opinion. The proposition that there is not a single liberal modernity, as insisted on by the consensus, but can exist in various national forms has far-reaching significance well beyond Hungary. Jan Patočka once wrote about the Great Czech and Little Czech traditions, meaning that occasionally small nations have the chance to play a major role on the European stage.

In November 1956, the director of the Hungarian News Agency, shortly before his office was flattened by artillery fire, sent a telex to the entire world with a desperate message announcing that the Russian attack against Budapest had begun. The dispatch ended with these words: "We are going to die for Hungary and for Europe."

Orbán has certainly made statements that can be read as a claim to be doing something analogous, to save Europe from liberalism and the liberal elites who are pushing Europe towards the abyss. It goes without saying that there are many who are incensed by the very idea of Orbán personally or Hungary generally doing any such thing – so much should be more than evident from the foregoing. All the same, I think it is safe to say that when the history of post-1989 Hungary comes to be written a generation from now, Viktor Orbán will be one of its protagonists. Maybe this will be true of Europe too.

References

Fenby, Jonathan. 2012. *The General: Charles De Gaulle and the France He Saved.* New York: Skyhorse Publishing.

Kundera, Milan. 1984. "The Tragedy of Central Europe", *New York Review of Books.* Volume 31, No.7, 26 April 1984.

Ober, Josiah. 2016. "Lessons of Demopolis", *Aeon.* https://aeon.co/essays/the-marriage-of-democracy-and-liberalism-is-not-inevitable?utm_content=bufferf5514&utm_medium=social&utm_source=twitter.com&utm_campaign=buffer

Patočka, Jan. 1996. *Mi a cseh?* [What is Czech?]. Pozsony: Kalligram.

Streeck, Wolfgang. 2016. "In jedem Einwanderungsland entstehen Enklaven", *Wirtschaftswoche,* 11 March 2016. http://www.wiwo.de/politik/deutschland/wolfgang-streeck-in-jedem-einwanderungsland-entstehen-enklaven/13304226-all.html

Wiedermann Helga. 2014. *Sakk és Póker: Krónika a magyar gazdasági szabadságharc győztes csatáiról* [Chess and poker: Chronicle about the winning battles of the Hungarian economic freedomfiht]. Budapest: Kairosz.

Hungary: the Fidesz Project[*]

It is hard to find a political cleavage line as deep as the one that divides left from right in Hungary. It has all the qualities of an ethnic polarisation, in the context of which each side attributes the worst to the other and, consequently, there is no dialogue between the two sides. At the deepest level, the divide is ontological, about what constitutes good and evil, what is the meaning of democracy, what is owed by members of society to one another. It is impossible to understand the dynamics of Hungarian politics without recognising that it is a politically segmented society. The polarisation is so far reaching that it can fairly be said to add up to a cold civil war. At the time of writing, the chances of a grand historic compromise look impossible, except that politics is the art of the possible, so the option should not be excluded entirely. It is worth noting here that a sizeable section of Hungarian society has become entirely disillusioned with politics; this creates a possibility for both left and right to mobilise once and future supporters by deploying an effective communications strategy.

The cleavage has well-established historical origins with its roots in the pre-First World War era when historic Hungary had taken major steps towards defining a national model of modernity, even if this model was very partial and was quite incapable of solving the problem of the peasantry, of the non-Magyar minorities or of developing something like

[*] Published online at *Aspen Review* https://www.aspenreview.com/article/2017/hungary%3A-the-fidesz-project.

a modern concept of citizenship (cf. republicanism in France after 1871). The failed revolutions of 1918–1919, Trianon and the loss of empire shattered the pre-1914 model of modernity and saddled Hungary with a minimally updated k.u.k model of elite rule. This model was stable to stagnant and was definitively destroyed by the Second World War. There were stumbling attempts to relaunch the quest for a Hungarian modernity after the war, but these were quashed by the communist takeover; and much the same happened to the incipient model of modernity embodied in the 1956 revolution (which was a revolution, despite the widespread preference for calling it an uprising, see Heller). The post-1956 system was sustained by far-reaching coercion and the threat of coercion, but did accept some limits to power thanks to the memory of the failed revolution, which had, after all, scattered the Stalinist nomenklatura to the four winds in a matter of days.

What the Kádárist regime did was to entrench the power of the nomenklatura and to promote a kind of weak two-way relationship based on consumerism. But the relationship was always one of dependence by the many on the few and instead of overseeing the transformation of the traditional peasantry into modern citizenship, it kept the bulk of the population in a status of tutelage. In some ways, Kádárism was an ironic reprise of the interwar system, in which a narrowly based, traditionally legitimated elite (in the Weberian sense) blocked the emergence of a modern civic-minded society.

Kádárism did much the same, except that it was legitimated by reference to an increasingly unsustainable ideology, by the power of the Soviet Union as the ultimate guarantor of communism, by Kádár's personality and by consumerism. When these failed, the system failed. And the failure took place in slow motion, which allowed the nomenklatura to regroup, preempt the chances of a revolution in 1989 (cf. Czechoslovakia or Estonia) and to entrench as much of its power as it could in the brave new world of electoral democracy, but without creating anything resembling an all-encompassing democratic infrastructure. It was with these antecedent processes that the Republic of Hungary was launched in 1989–1990. Perhaps nothing shows the extent and depth of the carry-over from the previous system, the absence of anything resembling a caesura, as the decision to amend the 1949 Stalinist Constitution rather than write a new one.

It was an inauspicious start to democracy that was made worse by the lack of skills of the first democratically elected government under the prime minister, József Antall, and the success of the salvaging activity of the nomenklatura. The next crucial step was the recognition that the technocrats of the communist era, the democratic opposition and many of the heirs of the nomenklatura had a good deal in common, above all, maybe, their conviction that they and they alone had the right to rule the country. The 1990 election result, which produced a centre-right majority, was – on this view – not just an aberration, but flouted the will of history – the communist years had left many with the belief that somehow or other history was, really, truly, law-governed after all; and it was on their side.

The Rise of the Liberal Consensus

The next step was the rise of the liberal consensus in the 1990s (Mouffe). The post-communist left in Hungary was looking for a home that reached beyond Hungarian society, which could assure it a support base, because the left always knew that its domestic support was insecure. It could win elections if a centre-right government had failed *and* (not *or*) if it was capable of mounting a convincing communications strategy, relying on the confusion of the relatively unsophisticated Hungarian voter. The semantic and cognitive skills of the latter were improving slowly, thanks to the change of generations and to experience, but were certainly low in the 1990s. Hence support from abroad became crucial to sustain the left's legitimacy and its self-legitimation by the 2000s.

The encounter with the liberal consensus was, thus, a fruitful one, at any rate in the short term in giving meaning to a leftwing identity in the aftermath of the collapse of communism. But it had its downside in the longer term – it made it possible for the post-communist left to evade having to redefine its identity, not to ask questions about what being leftwing meant in a democratic system in which it was competing with other currents and to reflect on its responsibility for the communist years.

This absence of a redefinition, thanks to the international context, had the consequence that the Hungarian left, aided and abetted by the remnants of the communist nomenklatura, inherited a great deal from the one party system intellectually and culturally, in terms of values and attitudes, as well as physically (in the form of property, networks, money). Crucially, it saw itself as a hegemonic elite endowed with a transcendental mission of transforming Hungarian society according to its vision of modernity, a vision that was defined overwhelmingly by the leftwing elite's understanding of what the West was and wanted. Inevitably, given that this was an instrumental endeavour, the West so constructed was narrowly defined by the uses to which the elite in question wanted to put it; in effect what we are looking at is an "imagined West" (in Anderson's language). And predictably it had less and less to do with actual Hungarian realities, whether in sociological terms (stratification, income distribution, poverty, gender roles, urban-rural cleavages, population movements etc.) or in the light of the aspirations of Hungarian society, which while in no way post-material did include non-material elements, like the meanings and security of a collective identity.

What is striking about this elite, which continues to dominate Budapest cultural life, though this is less true of the provinces (which this elite rather despises anyway), is that it failed (and still fails) to recognise that it has become a comprador elite. It has functioned in such a way as to inhibit cultural creativity by its feigned or real indifference to innovation, to the great diversity of the West, to the significance of globalisation (like Black Swans, cf. Taleb) and, maybe most importantly, that in a democracy the role of the intellectual has changed irreversibly from its role as moral legislator to interpreter (Bauman). The left-liberal elite in Hungary performs none of these roles or only very marginally so at best.

One of the politically significant features of the Hungarian left has been its propensity to corruption. The 2002–2010 governments were widely recognised as having come close to establishing a rentier system, in which the resource was not a raw material, like oil or natural gas, but taxpayers' money and whatever moneys could be siphoned off from EU cohesion and structural funds.

This is the cultural and political context of the last two decades. It is against this background that the leftwing and centre-right governments of the 2002–2012 should be assessed. Fidesz successfully reconstructed the centre-right around its core ideas of conservatism and Christian Democracy, solidarity, family, nationhood and statehood, with the underlying imperative of (finally) establishing a model of modernity that was in tune with historically inherited traditions, social aspirations and democracy (Oltay). It is crucial to understand that Fidesz has always had a clear commitment to Europe, but that this did not mean invariably accepting what the European Commission decided.

Neo-conservatives vs. Neo-nomenklatura

The task of the centre-right was always going to be a hard one in the aftermath of communism. What, after all, did it mean that one was a conservative when the relevant past to be conserved was the communist one from which the conservatives sought to distance themselves? Likewise, how could one (re)define Christian Democracy when a sizeable section of society was secular and had rather negative associations with organised religion, seeing that the churches had been heavily penetrated by the communists? In a very real sense, post-communist conservatism had to be radical in order to re-establish itself as conservative – a paradox that haunted the 1990–1994 government. Fidesz regrouped the right around a set of values that were not so strongly past-orientated, that took on the agenda of modernity derived from Hungarian resources and which understood that it could be radical towards the neo-nomenklatura and retain its centre-right credentials. In one important respect Fidesz was helped by the left. The espousal of neo-liberal market fundamentalism by the left allowed Fidesz to proclaim the importance of the state as an instrument of solidarity, redistribution and security.

The left, given the polarisation, contested each and every one of these values and did so vociferously, all too often gravely distorting what the Fidesz government was actually seeking to achieve. It is not unfair to suggest that the left's concept of opposition was to aim at the destruction of the centre-right, to delegitimate it completely and somehow to secure a political hegemony for itself to parallel the cultural hegemony that it believes that it already enjoys. It follows logically that in this belief system, the left can have no theory of a democratic centre-right and, likewise explains the widely propagated assertion that the centre-right was much the same as the far-right.

By 2010, the economic mismanagement by the Gyurcsány and Bajnai governments had brought the country into a parlous situation. Not only had Hungary become heavily indebted, but the machinery of the state was in complete disarray – it barely functioned. So, for example, the police had been very largely withdrawn from rural areas, thereby providing the space for far-right vigilante activity. The taxation system had become wholly haphazard as a result of the constant changes introduced by the government in a vain attempt to shore up its finances, and tax morale hit new lows. Bajnai's austerity package brought new strata closer to the poverty line and created fertile ground for far-right agitation. The unresolved Roma issue added to this, especially in the northeast Hungarian rust-belt. Outmigration was on the increase, notably in the medical profession. EU membership facilitated this. In effect, whoever had won the 2010 elections would have had to introduce major and deep-seated reforms.

Fidesz won a two-thirds majority, and Viktor Orbán, the prime minister, interpreted this as a mandate for a radical transformation and proceeded to act along these lines. These reforms should have been introduced after the regime shift of 1989, but were neglected by the left because it would have been to their disadvantage; the Antall government lacked the capacity to launch anything far-reaching; and the 1998–2002 Fidesz-led government only began the reforms but was unable to complete them.

Fidesz's task in 2010 was a major one. In effect, what had come into being after the collapse of communism was a Hungarian version of the "deep state", the Turkish *derin devlet*, in which the state administration may be competent and skilled technically, but what it administers is not what the (elected) government instructs it to do. So from the outside, what one sees looks like a Weberian legal-rational bureaucracy, but the reality lies elsewhere. The public servants are serving not the public, but their political masters from whom they expect protection, advancement, status and access to state funds for private purposes. Note that the state machinery includes the administration of justice.

A version of this deep state was constructed by the nomenklatura before and above all after 1989. The colour of the government could change, but that did not mean that a politically independent public function would come into being. And as the years passed, new entrants were rapidly socialised into the norms of the deep state or they were excluded or were silenced if they remained inside (Hirschman).

To that may be added the two central problems of any modern state administration, its size and its autonomy over society. Weber's thinking was informed by his analysis of a relatively small bureaucracy, but the modern state is much larger and has a critical mass that makes it all but impossible for political supervision to function effectively (Mann, Nordlinger). This state of affairs enhances the ability of any bureaucracy to establish tacit targets of its own, its own survival being the most important, that may be at odds with both the political strategy of the government and the *bonum publicum*. If we add the nomenklatura element to this mix, we can see that the Fidesz project had a formidable task if it wanted to implement its radical reform programme. It would have to create an entirely new state apparatus. Predictably this generated resentment and resistance on the part of those affected.

Hungarian solution to Hungarian problems

In brief, in 2010, a broad front transformation strategy was elaborated by the new government. Its economic strategy, however, was less than successful. In sum, it was a growth strategy based on the assumption that by 2012 the European and global economy would have recovered sufficiently to pull Hungary along with it; this turned out to be a misjudgement and that, in turn, was further exacerbated by the unexpected harshness with which the Commission treated the Hungarian deficit, threatening to cut cohesion funds (this did not happen in the end, but caused resentment especially as Spain was handled with kid gloves), only to accept grudgingly that the deficit would be within the required three percent for 2013.

Government debt was still high but was brought down from somewhere over 90 percent to below 80 percent – still high, but heading in the direction of manageability. It was a central tenet of Orbán's that austerity should fall not on the shoulders of the consumer, but the service sector and the multinationals. This was very unpopular in many circles, predictably. Other reforms targeted the tax system, secondary and higher education, the governance of religious establishments, small and medium-sized enterprises, the justice system, local government and the public administration. The last sought to breathe new life into the top-heavy, complex and frequently user-hostile bureaucracy which was all too often a drag on entrepreneurialism, as well as being a seed-bed of corruption.

Probably the two most controversial changes were the new Basic Law and the media law. They both attracted the most extreme and most ill-founded criticism. Two examples. It was widely claimed that the new Constitution banned abortion; it did not. Equally, it was claimed that by changing the name of the country to "Hungary" from the "Republic of Hungary", the new Constitution had thereby changed the form of the state; line three of the Constitution reads, "the Hungarian state is a republic". There were countless other instances of ignorance and deliberate misinterpretation, aided and abetted by the opposition which had

excellent connections with the international media. The Constitutional Court, which had been supposedly emasculated, repeatedly declared
laws unconstitutional, thereby demonstrating that the checks and balances of the system were working adequately.

It was as if domestic and international commentators were vying
among themselves as to who could dream up the most extreme instances of these purported attacks by the Orbán government on democracy.
The German-language press went furthest in this campaign. The *Süddeutsche Zeitung* in its edition of the 1 May 2010, that is, just a few days after Fidesz's electoral victory, but before it actually announced any polic-
es, declared that Hungary had a Fascist government.

This demands an explanation. In brief, the Fidesz government offend-
ed against the sacralised canons of the left-liberal consensus in several
ways. First, its two-thirds majority was an intolerable affront to those
who believed that history had ended in the victory of liberal democracy (as they understood it). Second, Fidesz's reform programme directly
contradicted conventional thinking and thereby threatened to revitalise
the opposition to the liberal consensus from the right, something that
the consensus believed was already on the scrapheap of history. Thirdly,
there were the generally leftwing presuppositions and assumption-sets of
the bulk of the media, who were predictably predisposed to believe the
worst reading of whatever the Fidesz government did. Fourth was and is
Central Europe's discursive deficit, that whatever was said in Hungarian (Czech, Polish, Estonian etc.) carried much less weight than English or French. Fifth, the insights of postcolonial theory tell us that power relations within Europe are uneven and that large polities, especially
those with a colonial past, have a tendency to insist that only their way
is correct and that smaller states are deviant when they behave differently. Finally, there is the half-explicit universalist ideology of the liberal consensus, that there is a single humanity and in so far as there isn't,
there should be one—the slide from the descriptive to the prescriptive is
so slick as to escape the eye. In effect, the consensus does not accept its
own contingency, implicitly denies that it too is a product of history and

believes that its values cannot be challenged by a state that is in Europe and is a member of the European Union. Fidesz, by rejecting this universalism and insisting on a specifically Hungarian solution to Hungarian problems, was guilty of the unpardonable sin of going against the laws of history.

The Fidesz reform programme is far from over. Whatever its fate, the challenges to it at home and abroad have nothing to do with constructive criticism, but are aimed at burying it, at treating it as dangerous anomaly and making the world safe for the consensus. Bauman's moral legislation lives on. Hungary under Fidesz is a constant challenge to this project, hence the unremitting campaign to eliminate it.

An Epistemological Crisis*

W hat we are looking at is far more than an economic crisis and far more than a crisis of European integration, even if much of the analysis chooses to explore it from this perspective. While the perspective is valid in itself, it has the consequence of hiding other processes – political, cultural, sociological – that affect the crisis and, by ignoring them or not identifying them, we make the solution of the crisis less likely. In short, deep seated changes are taking place in Europe and some of these are partly accelerated by the economic crisis, which has exposed the fragility of Western material well-being. It is in this sense that the word crisis is appropriate – social realities are increasingly out of alignment with institutions and elite thinking.

The crisis has also brought into question the reliability of both state and market as the central organising principle of Western democracy. After 1945, a great deal of trust was invested in the state as rational redistributor and allocator, as well as the ultimate source of rationality. By the late 1970s, this was being questioned and the dysfunctions of the state were to be eliminated by the market. The market, therefore, gradually came to be seen as a competing source of rationality, one that trumped the state in an increasing number of areas. Note here that whereas as the state is and must be a political category, the market is understood as free of politics and is a primarily economic process, albeit culture, psychology

---

* Originally published in Jensen, Jody and Ferenc Miszlivetz, *Reframing Europe's Future: Challenges and failures of the European construction*. London: Routledge, 2014, 718.

and other factors are now recognised as forming a part of market behaviour. What this elevation of the market to paramountcy ignored, however, were and are the political implications of the shift, that this effectively amounted to abandoning politics and political inputs into the central processes of society. Democracy was thereby reduced to something narrower, almost to being a spectator with few legitimate points to make. At the same time, the functioning of the market was naturalised and to some extent sacralised. The supreme rationality of the market ruled and was above and beyond questioning; those who did raise objections were dismissed as "irrational" or as "dinosaurs" or "reactionaries".

What the foregoing suggests, and suggests strongly, is that it is not sufficient to see the crisis as either an economic or a political or even a sociological one, even if all these spheres are out of alignment with how they are widely understood, but crucially that Europe is in the grip of an epistemological crisis, above all where the elites are concerned.

In summary form, an epistemological crisis can be identified when the assumptions and discourses of a particular normativity, of a plausibility structure sustained by an elite, are out of alignment with the way in which other elites construct the world and, vitally, the social support enjoyed by the counter-elite is real and cogent. The most salient and influential such elite is the one that has accepted and internalised liberal values and regards these values as the supreme embodiment of both rationality and morality. This is the liberal consensus of our times. Hence those inside the liberal consensus repeatedly find themselves in contradictions that they do not, indeed cannot recognise and when the evidence of their contradictory position is presented to them, they wave it away or ignore it.

In this instance, the cognitive world constructed by the liberal consensus cannot adequately fathom the qualities of the decorrelation and dealignment that Europe is in, a world where political elites pursue normative goals that do not correspond to, let alone respond to the aspirations of society. The rising inequality, fear of economic deterioration, of the uncontrollable impact of globalisation and the inter-generational crisis may be the most central here. Indeed, even the term "society" may be a misnomer, given the fragmentation of power. All of which should make it clear that those inside the consensus cannot grasp adequately why things have gone wrong and, consequently, still prescribe policies that either do nothing (at most little) or exacerbate the crisis.

The explanation that can help to clarify this state of affairs is that the liberal consensus may well have started out life as relatively open. The proposition that the "best of left and right" traditions would generate a set of norms that would suit the conditions in Europe after the collapse of communism was persuasive and certainly helped to give the left a new lease of life by ending its suspicion of the market, as well as burying its long standing penchant for nationalisation. What was less predictable was that in a relatively short period of time, a decade and a half, the consensus would evolve into an ideology and that, in turn, acquired the qualities of an identity. Identities do, of course, change over time, but in this instance, there was precious little incentive for change, especially as the neo-conservative embrace of market fundamentalism, that markets solve everything, coincided with the left's pro market turn. The two – neo-conservatism and the consensus – imperceptibly merged their different approaches, not least because the left had abandoned its traditional critical stance towards the market, which then gave market-mindedness a near monopoly; certainly it was a hegemony that Gramsci would have recognised.

The principal characteristics of epistemological closure, as argued, is that those inside the box are persuaded of their correct views, do not admit alternatives, regard those who emerge with counter-arguments as tiresome and certainly not as worthy adversaries and, perhaps most significantly in the current context, is their propensity to grow more and more introverted and conservative (in the sense of rejecting innovation and even change). In other words, closure appears to be dynamic.

It follows, that those so affected will tend to interpret events, change, processes, phenomena according to their epistemological criteria and this generally means that there is an ever greater distance between what the sociological reality happens to be and what those inside the closure think it is. There is, then, a cognitive gap.

What is notable about the liberal consensus is the constant proclamation of its openness, its commitment to diversity, to multiculturalism, to innovation and to a strong, normative concept of a single humanity. In reality, liberal consensus is increasingly nothing of the kind where openness is concerned. As it condenses its discourses, it correspondingly closes itself off from the ideas, process or inputs that might challenge or undermine its cherished ideology. Hence what we are looking at in sociological reality is not a commitment to openness etc., but to a targeted openness and so on. The consensus is open to some, but far from all; indeed intuitively I have the sense that it is less open now than it was a decade ago, but these things are hard to prove. This propensity to target specific objectives, to privilege some social groups over others, demonstrates that the universalism of the consensus is not as universal – driven by the vision of a single humanity – as it would like to claim.

A particular and rather successful instrument wielded by the protagonists of the consensus is "politically correct" language. Clearly an aspect of insisting on morality over politics, PolKorr (the association with Marxist-Leninist usage is quite deliberate) allows the consensus to silence discordant and dissenting voices without having to put forward an argument. It is taken to be self-evident and that's it. This does not, of course, mean that those holding these views stop thinking them, it's just that they are silenced. There is a more than ghostly similarity here to communism – both are reflections of monistic thought-worlds. The politically noteworthy difference is that there is no vanguard party to act as enforcer, although social pressure can be just as effective, if not more so. But like all hegemonies, these thought-worlds tend to harden and carry within them the seeds of their own weaknesses. They tend to be anti-innovative, above all because they are inclined to see themselves as an end state ("end of history"). If only the champions of PolKorr were to read to Bakhtin and Lotman, they would know that sooner or later tightly defined systems become vulnerable to challenge from outside. We are some way from the challenge for the time being, however. What we have instead is a revitalisation of the universalist moral legislation dissected by Bauman. From the perspective of democracy as the exercise of power by the consent of the governed, two old-new problems arise. One is who has the right to define PolKorr, indeed the entirety of the liberal consensus, how can significant swathes of opinion be simply be excluded (as "populist" or "xenophobic" or whatever) from the democratic debate? The other is that of the *quis custodiet*, who has oversight of the liberal elite to prevent the excesses? What we are looking at is, indeed, an elite construct, which – whether we approve or not – is cultural and not open to debate with a range of alternative views. Here it is worth adding that no plausibility structure lives for ever and the more tightly it is constructed, the more it moves towards monology (Bakhtin again), the more it lays itself open to a dramatic collapse.

Possibly the most damaging aspect of this is the readiness to shout "racism" whenever one of the groups favoured by the liberal consensus comes in for criticism. There is a twofold problem here – the simultaneous denial and acceptance of collective representation and the transmission of the verbal weapon to the affected group that whatever happens to them is the result of "racism" (the racism of the majority), with the result that the group in question acquires a greatly simplified concept of causation, and one in which it has no responsibility, or agency for which responsibility is assumed. One response to this is radicalisation.

The liberal consensus has not, I would suggest, reached the stage of Mary Douglas's enclave culture which erects a "wall of virtue" around itself and rigidly excludes everything that does not conform. Bakhtin's monology also resembles this. What can be said, however, is that some adherents of the consensus are tending in the enclave direction.

The characteristics of this particular closure are broadly structured by a commitment to human rights, democracy, the support of immigrant minorities and the LGBT community, gender equality and to a rather more muted extent, the disabled. In all these cases, the definition of the category is entirely in the hands of those inside the closure and in acting as a reality defining agency, they are active in seeking to impose their reality definitions on others. Because these categories are part of a monistic system, its members can readily ignore precedents, parallels or inconsistencies that might undermine the closure. In truth, this closure is political, so that political interests and power will override external inputs that might threaten the solidity of the closure.

This can happen even when the exercise of this power goes counter to the purported values of the system – the commitment to openness is maybe the one abused most flagrantly, seeing that a closure by definition is antagonistic to new ideas, external inputs, different logics and, indeed, to alterity. In brief, the proclaimed principles and ideals of the closure, despite the assumptions to the contrary, are not universal, but are targeted at whatever suits the political aims of the members of the closure. And it goes without saying, or should, that the selection criteria of what is targeted are firmly under the control of the insiders.

There are further consequences resulting from the crisis. Liberalism, being a lineal descendant of the universalist aspirations of the European Enlightenment, always did have trouble with collective identities. In the Enlightenment scheme of things, these were destined to fade away as a transcendental universe of reason – one that invariably resembled the assumptions of those putting these ideas forward – would triumph over petty particularities. Nothing of the kind happened, of course, and even in the heyday of Enlightenment thought, there were counter-arguments and proposals put forward to challenge these assumptions, Herder's being the most obvious, for which he has been excoriated as a proto-fascist ever since. The entire history of modern nations (which are completely different from states, whatever current English usage ordains) refutes the assumption, but then those in the grip of a transcendental normativity seldom bother with evidence that undermines one's case.

If we fast-forward to the 1990s, the consensus imperceptibly took another step, this time about collectivities. Its protagonists, influenced no doubt by the "end of history" argument, concluded that, hurray, finally these tiresome collective identities were finished and the dawn or midmorning of universalism had arrived. This coincided with the unipolar moment, that brief decade when the US appeared to be in possession of the agenda of the world; I'm not saying propter hoc here, but the coincidence in time is suggestive. The consensus simply integrated the *ought* into the *is*, that collective identities should fade and, actually, they had faded. The shift from referring to states as nations simply mirrored this, consciously or not.

This shift can clearly be seen as a move into unreality, something that is generally evident when a sizeable number of people confuse the *sein* and the *sollen*, the *is* and the *ought*. In effect, and this is a further reason why it is proper to refer to an epistemological crisis, the reality that collective identities were alive and well just could not be decoded by the categories available to the consensus. Matters grew worse when it emerged that these collective identities were not only prospering, but that they were able to go on generating political and cultural power. In the context of the EU, the rise of intergovernmentalism and the nation-state interest were clear enough. Outside Europe, as with China for example, the consensus had little to say other than make disapproving noises. In a way, the inability of liberalism to find an answer to nationhood and other identity collectives is its greatest weakness, one that it cannot acknowledge, even if there is perfectly respectable national liberal alternative around. Yes, but that throws the universalism out the window and that is unacceptable, because that would force the consensus to acknowledge that the project of turning the rest of the world into etiolated imitations of the West had failed, failed in spades as a matter of fact.

In this perspective, the West's love of moral legislation for the rest of the world lives on as an aspect of the consensus, it is encountering increasing resistance and is refusing to accept this resistance. This is yet another facet of the crisis. The universalism and the moral legislation are imposed within Europe as well, of course, and here the resistance is dismissed as populism, a word that currently means little more than "something that I don't like" (and can't fathom as to why it attracts a growing number of votes). Much the same problem is posed by religion, above all the slow realisation that outside Europe, religion remains a powerful force and inside, religiousness – including believing without belonging – may be on the increase.

What does follow from the foregoing is that liberalism, as currently understood, tends to see these collective identities as deviant or, the worst-case scenario, as proto-fascist or even crypto-fascist. Note that the term "fascist" has nothing to do with historical fascism à la Mussolini, but has become a generic word of condemnation in the liberal vocabulary. And precisely because it has been torn from its historical roots, it can be applied freely to any phenomenon or process that the user dislikes.

Another aspect of the epistemological crisis can be found in the strikingly contradictory view of the state in the assumptions of liberal universalism. As liberals, they are hostile to etatism and believe that individual interactions are sufficient to ensure whatever it is that liberal universalism wants to ensure – life, the universe and everything, I suppose. In their moral legislative role, on the other hand, the same reality-defining agency looks to the state to enforce moral regulation. An incontrovertible example is the way in which legal instruments are used to punish Holocaust denial and anything that can be squeezed into the category of hate speech – a category that is necessarily subjective and flexible. It also has the advantage that it can be made retroactive and thereby rewrite the past.

On the other hand, as a counter-move, the sections of society that do not identify with this universalising morality try to find refuge elsewhere. They can do this in a variety of ways, the most obvious of which is the opportunity structure provided by democracy – to vote for another party, one that does not espouse the moralising. The universalists respond by labelling them "populist" and endow populism with all the qualities of darkness that they can muster – notably that they are intolerant, racist, xenophobic and so on. What this labelling rather misses, however, is the linkage between populist and people, that by demonising the populists, they also, not all that indirectly, demonise the people. And that raises very interesting questions about the kind of democracy that the universalists favour, one without people, presumably, because people have this pesky habit of harbouring aspirations at variance with those of the universalising elites.

Anti-politics

Not least, this raises the problem of anti-politics. Anti-politics is, in brief, about creating a political world in which there is no further conflict, because the overwhelming majority are agreed on the basic principles of what is "good", that is, the moral content of the elite belief system has been integrated by society. Both the criteria of deciding what is good and their application have come together in a kind of unity. Because notionally there is such wide-ranging agreement, there are no serious problems with the elite-led quality of this idealised system. Note that here too the *sein* and the *sollen* are seriously confused. Anti-politics however mixes the ideals of the few with the aspirations of the many, but being elite-led, despises the latter, hence the charges of populism.

At the institutional level, left and right seem to be in broad agreement on this. Many decisions – as we shall see – are outsourced to legal, to technocratic, to bureaucratic decision making, to NGOs, to the market and so on. In all of these areas of power, conflict is either concealed or it is settled opaquely or it is declared non- conflictual, thereby adding to the spaces of depoliticisation. From the liberal elite's perspective, in real rather than rhetorical terms, this is advantageous because it allows the liberal ethos to reign and rule unchallenged – it is unchallenged because the possible modes of challenge have been marginalised.

In political reality, because this system of thought does not enjoy hegemony, let alone monopoly, it is imposed with strong discursivity by an elite that sees itself as a Leninist vanguard, albeit it has no Cheka to back it up, even if it would vigorously reject the analogy. But the evidence, if not compelling, is at least thought-provoking. The entire edifice of the PolKorr imposes a language and a form of thinking that cannot, may not be deconstructed. Attempts to do so are ignored or shouted down and those who adopt this line of argument are in effect expelled from the general conversation. The outcome is that the range of political action is curtailed, just as it was under communism. Of course there are substantial differences, there are no Gulags, no all-pervasive secret police, secret courts, even if surveillance is intensifying all the time. Still, where the analogy holds is in the depoliticisation. Under communism, the party had a monopoly of political decision making. In the realm of the liberal consensus, there are indeed inputs from a wide variety sources, but the fundamentals of the system are tabooised and thus placed beyond questioning. To anyone who knows the contours of late communism, there are enough similarities for this to be alarming.

So the question can be put in this way, can one have politics without conflict? Yes, if we are in the grip of myths of social harmony, that the conflict-free unity of all is almost there. The very different reality is a nuisance, but can be overcome with a little effort etc. This, it would appear, is the underlying normativity of the liberal consensus.

The state

All states are not alike, they never were, and the same is true for polities and political systems. This is important, because it means that there is no political monoculture as yet, so that alternatives can be found and used as counter-examples. The liberal consensus prefers to look the other way when these counter-examples are cited or to treat them as temporary anomalies. Real alternatives are not permissible, they cannot be in a thought-world governed by a single mode of discourse, the moral monism so feared by Isaiah Berlin among others.

Yet what the liberal consensus appears unable to notice is that it is under challenge not only from those who would argue that democracy cannot be reduced to a single ordering principle – the particular hegemonic variant of liberalism now current – but also from those who are either indifferent to democracy or are hostile to it. These latter forces are weakening the state in ways that are recognised at the empirical level but are seldom seen as a part of the crisis of the state. We can begin from the narrative of the Weberian state, that the state controls the monopoly of violence within its frontiers, that there is a uniform distribution of authority and that the state is the ultimate source of rationality.

Globalisation, however, has begun to erode this model of the state, meaning that it is less effective in taxing, listing, and controlling the population than previously. In effect, growing numbers are escaping the purview of the state as refugees, migrants, neo-nomads, including high status migrants; tax nomads, tax shelters are reducing the income of the state and cyberspace is eroding the role of the state as a source of rationality. What we are seeing is a process where high status economic actors have moved beyond the control of even high capacity Western states, mimicking the low status nomads and migrants who are doing likewise. The irony is that the ideology of liberal consensus, with its privileging the freedom of the market, helps to sustain this environment. To the liberals may be added the libertarians who regard the state as a form of theft, a phenomenon admittedly more common in the US than in Europe.

James C. Scott in his *The Art of Not Being Governed* identifies a social and political process to the effect that sections of the population heavily burdened by the exactions of the state would move beyond its reach. His area of investigation is, broadly, the hill country between Nagaland and western China, but his insight can be applied to contemporary conditions (of which he may or may not approve). Whereas historically it was primarily people who moved to escape the state, and this was as true of Europe and Russia as of South-East Asia, with globalisation this has been the behaviour of capital.

What is noteworthy about this worldwide process of capital escaping the control of the taxing and supervising state is that it fits neatly into all the assumptions of interest maximisation and rationality. It is entirely rational for a corporation to establish a tax regime that ensures that it does not pay tax on the profits that it generated in a high or medium tax jurisdiction when there are others with very low or even zero tax rates, that is, the offshore tax shelters. This may be hard on the state and its citizens, but as long as it is legal, the corporation does not have to worry. The market is king, and all issues of ethics are subordinate to interest maximisation.

Several points are worth making here. First, there is the grand historical irony that it was Marx and the communists who proclaimed the withering away of the state, yet it is capitalism – some call it vulture capitalism – that is doing the real damage. Second, those who remove their (vast) legal profits from the control of the democratic state are no different structurally from the Russian and other former Soviet oligarchs who are doing likewise. The difference lies in how the money was acquired in the first place, by more or less legal activities in Western democracies and by blatant asset stripping in the former Soviet Union. Third, the money making industry sees to it that there is next no trickle down, at best there are the jobs in the finance and ancillary industries, which ends up as something not wholly unlike Russian-style asset stripping, except that it is legal though hideously complex, but does in real terms mean the steady siphoning off of the assets of those not in the finance industry, like the savings of the middle classes. Fourth, in a peculiar kind of way the process described here mimics civil society or, to be more accurate, brings into being semi-civil and uncivil society. It is semi-civil, because it is legal or at least at the margins of legality or it can be regarded as uncivil because it cares nothing for the rest of society.

Then, this market generated autonomous capital has acquired considerable political power that it uses to ensure that states do not impose regulations that would curtail their activities. All sites of power do something analogous, but what makes this different is that bases of this power are already beyond the limits of the state and are based on weak states that lack the capacity to supervise them. Short of reimposing colonial rule, something that liberalism and capital would do everything to prevent anyway, there is very little that the affected democratic states can do, but the issue does raise interesting questions about state sovereignty and whether it can be sustained in its present form. The process points towards another factor. The protagonists of the market argue their case in economic terms, but what we have seen in the last two decades is that economic power will generally be converted into political, in order not least to secure the reproduction of the system that gave rise to this new-found political power in the first place. It should be added to the foregoing that capital does continue to engage with the state, and does so from a significantly more powerful position than in the past.

The primary aim of this engagement is, as argued, that regulation on the free movement of capital and the autonomy of the sector should be as light as possible. To this end, those in the sector have developed a discourse and have established the ancillary support system – lobbies, PR firms, accountants, financial advisors – to deploy the discursivity and to give it legitimacy. Overcoming the activities of regulators, the finding of loopholes and so on, is a key dimension of this. Not least, given the rewards, the sector has been able to cream off a sizeable section of the talented and is regularly able to outfox the state. The state, broadly speaking, has been unable to meet this challenge to its power and equally importantly to its capacity and effectiveness. The reality that the actions of the capital sector erode, if not actually undermine citizenship by creating massive disparities, means that democracy itself is threatened. The rise of so-called populist parties is one consequence, as we have seen.

At the same time, the state is still ultimate guarantor of legality and the legal system, of property, and of contracts. It sustains a legal system that is necessary for the continued functioning of the system. This creates a striking tension between the two, that capital disdains the state, but uses it for its purposes and blackmails it by the too big to fail argument. This contradiction too is a part of the epistemological crisis that the liberal consensus must deal with, because society suffers as a result through its disempowerment.

All the foregoing, the dissection of the role of capital, should be seen in the overall context of this argument, that Europe is grappling with an epistemological crisis. The activity of capital has created patterns that are gravely weakening the equality of citizenship, including the civic solidarity and trust without which citizenship is worth little. On the other hand, the hegemonic discourses mask this sociological and political reality. The intellectual toolkit of the liberal consensus cannot deal with this and analogous phenomena. Interestingly, the somewhat tepid revival of curiosity about Marx and his analysis of capitalism has yet to produce anything that might represent a breakthrough in thinking. And the European left that feels itself at home in the embrace of the liberal consensus, abandoned its belief in Marxism far too recently to be comfortable with it again, quite apart from the intellectual failure, as well as much else, represented by the collapse of communism.

The return of evil

There is another dimension to this crisis that seldom receives much attention. The liberalism that we have today has basically abandoned its Enlightenment foundations in an unexpected fashion. Enlightenment rationality might have taken over great bundles of assumptions from Christianity – the central one being that history has a purpose, human betterment, and linearity – but in one crucial respect it also innovated. The banishing of evil also meant the abandonment of absolutes other than reason itself, but that was always too varied and contingent to function effectively as an absolute. This created a two centuries long space for liberalism to stand for tolerance and progress, implying that history has no end.

This abjuring of absolutes and denial of evil – evil cannot coexist with a faith in progress and continued human improvement – was quietly abandoned in the early 1990s. And it was certainly tacit, even if the response to Fukuyama's essay made a good deal of noise. There were several steps in this process. First, there was the collapse of communism, which eventually (a rather short eventually) left social democracy dangling, with nowhere to go.

The second was the helplessness of Western Europe when it came to dealing with the aftermath of communism. Dazzled by the peaceful transition almost everywhere, it had no answers to the collapse of Yugoslavia and, such was my personal experience, was not ready to listen to arguments that might have prevented the mass killing. The implication is that when confronted with what appeared inexplicable, how could the former Yugoslavs not respond to universal liberalism? The answer was "ancient hatreds" or "irrationality" or "ethnic entrepreneurs", all of them with the presence of evil just about discernibly behind them. No one formulated it in these terms at the time, after all, to have done so would have meant confronting the West's own haplessness.

The third step was the similarly silent proclamation of the Holocaust as absolute evil. This proved to be a major step. It rehabilitated evil as an accepted category in European thought and, at the same time, provided a firm answer to the challenge of post-modernity, that everything is text, that we do not have even rationality as a definitive and hard system by which to orientate our lives. If there is evil, obviously, then universal reason has failed. And if there is absolute evil, then logically there must also be lesser evil.

Liberalism took on these categories of thought, again more tacitly than anything else, and this reception proved to be something of a liberation from the dilemma enunciated by Isaiah Berlin, the problem of incommensurability of some values. Equally, it put paid to John Gray's agonistic liberalism. It achieved this by allowing liberalism to target certain values as positive and others as negative, not actually declaring them "evil", but the underlying assumption set was there. It also made liberal universalism more focused and allowed West Europeans to acknowledge their colonial pasts, with profuse apologies, but to side-step the problem of unequal power relations whether as between the West and "the rest" or, equally, as between European states and cultures. The danger of moral monism that this shift represented was not noticed or was ignored or dismissed, even though – as Isaiah Berlin made this amply clear – it was precisely this moral monism that was responsible for Soviet totalitarianism.

The bounded universalism of the consensus further created opportunities to deal with the difficulty that social democracy could never solve – the flourishing of collective identities that are a constant impediment to universalism. In sum, as already noted, Western democratic collectivities have been declared to be "post- national", therefore their cultural particularities are benign, maybe folkloric, whereas the Central Europeans (and this is where we came in with Yugoslavia) are suspect, far more so than the West Europeans. Thus when a political movement (Scotland, Catalonia) seeks state independence, this is disliked, but not condemned in the terms reserved for the Central Europeans. There is no consistency in this. The sociological reality, that a discursively constructed identity that cannot be categorised as anything other than ethnic lives on in France or England or anywhere else in Western Europe is simply screened out.

Finally, the "hard" quality of the new evil made the liberal consensus much more operational than before. The superimposition of morality over politics was a further advantage, because it gave the consensus the method for ignoring tiresome issues like popular sovereignty and, the old dilemma, what happens when a political community opts for illiberalism, as it is currently doing in statistically (and politically) significantly numbers.

Thus the operationability of the consensus paradoxically produced a bounded universalism. Certain groups had the backing of the quietly redefined liberalism, like some minorities (immigrants, Roma, LGBT), but not others (historic and linguistic minorities, the losers of globalisation like the unskilled manual working class). The social exclusion of some was condemned, but that of others, like the traditional manual working class, could be ignored. Most interestingly, the slow decline of the economic security of the middle classes, coupled with the emergence of the super-rich and their ability to shift policies to their advantage, could be ignored.

The reality of this redistributive injustice seemingly troubled the consensus not at all. The new liberalism has opted for freedom over equality, is ignoring the tension that was at the heart of the left in the 1945–1991 era, and was not concerned with the consequences; conceivably this may have been an implicit reaction (an overreaction?) to the extreme unfreedom practised by communism and a sensibility that it was this that made the utopian project of the left impossible. The proposition that there could be an equality of freedom plays no role in this kind of thinking and that the ideal goal of "progressive" thought is to strive to maintain an equilibrium between the two is likewise absent. The outcome, the staggering inequalities and consequent limitations on freedom, has yet to be confronted. The consensus remains unimpressed, though it is now beginning to be aware of the political implications of redistributive injustice as the vote for those dismissed as "populists" has begun to rise throughout Europe.

The present inequalities are being reproduced, if not actually intensified, and, given current assumptions, this cannot even be perceived adequately. Furthermore, the new global structures make it impossible, or at least uniquely difficult to find a way out. In summary form, European modernity assumed that growth would persist and thereby secure permanent upward mobility and/or a steady incremental access to materials goods that would be passed on from one generation to the next. This assumption has come apart, sizeable sections of society are, at best, level pegging, but more likely facing a shrinking disposable income, a decline in their capital accumulation – social, cultural as well as material – and they are no longer able to transmit this to the next generation. In a word, progress is over; perhaps the word *progress* should be underlined here. If this proposition is even halfway accurate, and *ceteris paribus* this seems plausible, then all the major European political assumptions about a linear development towards a better future are best discarded. Radically new thinking is needed, but this is seldom available or, if it is offered, it is ignored.

References

Berlin, Isaiah. 1998. "Value pluralism" http://www.cs.utexas.edu/~vl/notes/berlin.html. Downloaded 28 December 2012.

Boyle, David. 2013. *Broke: who Killed the Middle Classes?* London: Fourth Estate.

Fukuyama, Francis. 2012. "The Future of History: Can Liberal Democracy Survive the Decline of the Middle Class?" *Foreign Affairs*, Vol. 91, No. 1 (JANUARY/FEBRUARY), 53-61.

Krastev, Ivan. 2010. "A Retired Power", *The American Interest*. July/August.

Malik, Kenan. 2000. "Let them die", *Prospect*, 20 November.

Mouffe, Chantal. 2005. "The 'End of Politics' and the Challenge of Right-wing Populism" in Francisco Panizza, *Populism and the Mirror of Democracy*. London: Verso.

Mulgan, Geoff. 2007. "Mary Douglas Remembered", *Prospect*, No.135.

Savoie, Donald J. 2010. *Power: where is it?* Montreal: McGill-Queen's University Press.

Schöpflin, George. 2012. *Politics, Illusions, Fallacies*. Tallinn: Tallinn University Press.

Scott, James C. 1998. *Seeing like a State: How Certain Schemes to Improve the Human Condition Have Failed*. New Haven: Yale University Press.

———. 2009. *The Art of Not Being Governed: an Anarchist History of Upland Southeast Asia*. New Haven: Yale University Press.

Taleb, Nassim Nicholas. 2007. *The Black Swan: the Impact of the Highly Improbable*. London, Penguin.

Townsend, Mark. 2011. "Searchlight poll finds huge support for far right 'if they gave up violence'", *The Guardian*. 27 February.

Urry, John. 2003. *Global Complexity*. Cambridge: Polity.

Orbán, Illiberalism*

Most commentators define "illiberalism" as a negative – often a strongly negative – version of liberalism, leaving the latter undefined. This is rather lazy or, at best, adds up to substituting moralising categories for analysis. In a word, illiberalism exists very largely in the eyes of the beholder – it is a series of attributions.

Some of this phenomenon is best explained by the profoundly negative charge triggered by the use of the word "illiberal", as Viktor Orbán did in his speech at Băile Tuşnad in 2014. This became a major symbolic event, although it is not in any sense certain that this was what Orbán intended. This was what he actually said:

> "[what we are] trying [is] to find the form of community organisation, the new Hungarian state, which is capable of making our community competitive in the great global race" [and] "*in this sense* the new state that we are constructing in Hungary is an illiberal state, a non-liberal state. It does not reject the fundamental principles of liberalism such as freedom [emphasis added]."

It is evident from even a cursory reading that the word "illiberal" referred to economic liberalism, to market fundamentalism, and, equally, that the classical principles of liberalism, fundamental rights, were not affected. But that was not how the word was interpreted, far from it. And

---

* Originally published online at https://revista22.ro/70271452/ce-este-iliberalismul.html.

it has been this distorted interpretation of illiberalism that has acquired the status of "fact", as well as giving liberalism a useful negative opposite by which to define itself.

In reality, any serious analysis of the Hungarian political system will show something different. The Fidesz government, and Orbán personally, have strong popular support and simultaneously the opposition is weak, divided and unable to construct a political formula that could challenge the Fidesz pre-eminence. The general elections of 8 April 2018 were clear evidence of this. Hence the Hungarian political scene can be described as segmented with one segment – the one that supports Fidesz – as dominant. By and large, once segmentation is established, it tends to endure.

Orbán has defined the Fidesz segment as the "central force-field", a project intended to dominate the intellectual discourse in Hungary, focusing on nationhood and conservative values. This central force-field is at the same time an open challenge to the liberal hegemony that rules the public conversation in much of Europe and, similarly, in the Hungarian opposition. It has, therefore, the aim of escaping the centre-periphery relationship that characterises much of European politics – the parity of esteem that supposedly underlies relations within the European Union is decidedly weak. It should be added that the force-field is far from cohesive. Voices critical of Orbán have emerged from the centre-right, not just the left. Jobbik has always been a radical opponent of Fidesz, of course.

The system that Orbán has constructed is marked by a number of features that flow from the ideas behind the segmentation, notably that it is the task of government to make provision for as wide a sector of the population as it can. For Fidesz, this has meant etatism, using the state to provide social protection against the vagaries of the market. The rising inequality in polities where the market is hegemonic is one of the areas where the Hungarian strategy is at odds with liberal mainstream thinking. Particularly noteworthy in this context is the problem of primitive capital accumulation in the semi-periphery. Fidesz has sought to resolve this through expanding state ownership. And it is worth adding that the experience of market domination under the leftwing governments (2002–2010) was disastrous. And even afterwards, the figures collated by Thomas Piketty show that between 2010 and 2016, the annual net outflow of capital from Hungary amounted to 7.2 percent of the gross domestic product, while transfers from the EU were 4.0 percent.

One aspect of the liberal critique of the Orbán system, which its opponents invariably call "regime", is that it has eroded or even destroyed checks and balances. This is certainly the view of a small, but noisy section of Hungarian civil society that has been attempting to play a surrogate opposition role and to mobilise support from the West. In reality, the evidence does not bear out this accusation.

The administration of justice functions adequately, judgements critical of the government are issued regularly and in the 2017–2019 EU's Justice Scoreboards Hungary emerged with reasonable markings, somewhere in the top third of the EU member states. The Constitutional Court, repeatedly misdescribed as having been eviscerated by the Orbán system, quashes laws frequently. In a recent interview, the president of the Court, Tamás Sulyok, stated that the Court "floats" above all three areas of power (legislature, executive and the judiciary).

There is extensive opposition criticism in both the print and electronic media; the most widely watched tv channels (RTL and ATV) are both critical of the government. Similarly, there are numerous websites that take an anti-Fidesz line and with around two-thirds of the population having access to electronic media (much higher in Budapest), charges of a centre-right information monopoly are wide of the mark. While there are around two dozen NGOs that insist on the autocratic character of the Orbán system, there are over 60,000 such bodies in Hungary, in other words it is a small minority of NGOs that takes this position. Street demonstrations are frequent and undisturbed by the authorities.

A word here about the Soros phenomenon. Soros has overtly sought to establish his liberal vision in Hungary, regardless of majority opinion, and has made extensive resources available to NGOs to achieve this. This raises a number of questions about the nature of democracy. NGOs are not elected, hence their legitimacy rests on output, on the validity of their critique of power. But it is very much open to question whether they can function as a surrogate opposition. To accept this proposition would mean that democracy can be divorced from popular sovereignty and values be substituted for the ballot box.

The trouble with this position is that it places considerable power in the hands of those who define these values and this power is not subject to accountability or, for that matter, to feed-back. Furthermore, if we accept that the Soros network has the right to operate as an externally-financed political actor in Hungary, then the same would apply to other sources of externally-driven activity, like that of Russia. Structurally there is no difference between what Soros is doing in Hungary and what Russia has done in the US presidential election, though naturally the content is quite different.

The Western liberal project, which defines itself partly against Orbán (and vice-versa), is overwhelmingly motivated by values as distinct from consensus and legitimacy. The emphasis on rule of law, while perfectly proper, does not seek to bring legality and legitimacy into alignment, but claims the right to formulate moral legislation (as identified by Zygmunt Bauman) and where necessary to use the power of the state to enforce the moral code.

This process can fly in the face of popular sovereignty, above all where the liberalism is engaged in social engineering against the preferences of the majority. Ultimately the conflict over values is sterile, because some values are negative (greed, mendacity, cruelty for example) and some are incommensurable (justice and mercy). More and more the conflict of values has come to resemble a religious struggle, with irreconcilable sacred spaces, meta-languages and belief systems. This leaves liberals and their national conservative opponents – the "illiberals" – engaged in a dialogue of the deaf.

In broad historic terms, we are in the midst of a political paradigm shift in Europe. The great liberal project of free markets and human rights has peaked. Around of a quarter of the population is committed to the project in the West – much less in Central Europe, maybe 10 percent – but a polarised opposition is gathering strength. There is a palpable weakening of the liberal mainstream.

In this context Hungary looks like a forerunner of the trend, in as much as it has stabilised the political field around a new national-conservative centre-right. Milan Kundera remarked (in his "Kidnapped Europe" essay) that one of the functions of Central Europe is to act as an early-warning system for Europe as a whole. This is what Hungary has demonstrated by accepting the rightward shift on the part of Fidesz. Unfortunately, few others received the message.

28 April 2018

Swings and Roundabouts? The Growing Gap between Western and Central Europe*

L et's assume that an alien, from Betelgeuse say, comes down to Earth to see how things are done there. He (she, it, ze, zo, zhe, zho whatever) would find it difficult to avoid coming to the conclusion that the European Union is in serious trouble and, equally, that those who are running it seem quite unable to recognise the crisis. To be precise, these are multiple, interlocking crises and they've been accumulating for a while. Some of these are global, like the Middle East, Russia and Ukraine; some are the EU's very own, like the intractable problem of the euro, Brexit and the future of Italy. To these may be added the slow, but unmistakeable transformation of the party system. Social Democracy is in meltdown, Christian Democracy has been infected by liberalism, liberalism itself has been captured from within by illiberal elements that have begun to resemble intransigent cultists and the voters are turning towards new rightwing and leftwing political movements. The adherents of the established parties dismiss these as "populism". But above them all looms the legitimation crisis, the EU's failure to provide an answer to the questions: why integrate and how to create accountability for the powers that have accumulated in Brussels.

To the former, the answers of the past – democracy, prosperity, open borders, peace – are largely exhausted, taken for granted. Even worse, while the EU does indeed offer a means of conflict resolution, this is in-

---

* Published in the *Hungarian Review*, Vol. IX, No.2. 2018, updated 2019.

creasingly being displaced by "human rights". Conflict resolution is central to all collectivities, given that asymmetries of power will always emerge, but what is to be done when the conflict resolver itself accumulates so much power that it becomes the source of asymmetry? This is where the EU can reasonably be located. The issue here is that effective conflict resolution requires a readiness to compromise and is focused on the particular problems of Europe, the latter – human rights – makes a universal moral claim and has a propensity to be absolute. Clearly, beyond a certain point the two are irreconcilable.

In these circumstances, the aforementioned alien would presumably have concluded that the EU had more than enough on its plate and, applying the rule of prudence, would not open another front, one where the likelihood of success was rather low. Yet – should we be surprised? – this precisely what the EU Commission has done.

Just before Christmas 2017, the EU Commission decided that it would launch an Article Seven procedure against Poland. If successful, Poland would be deprived of its voting rights in the EU and would generally find itself in a kind of quarantine until it mended its ways. Article Seven of the EU Treaty is widely referred to as the "nuclear option" in the armoury of the EU in the context of recalcitrant member states, that is, those where there is a serious threat to the basic values of the EU, as detailed in Article Two.

This is where the story gets complicated. First, Article Seven is almost impossible to implement, given the legal and political hurdles that its initiators have to jump. Besides, the entire point of a nuclear option is that it should never be used, but to establish a constraint. And the launching of the Article Seven procedure against Poland is bound to have unintended consequences. We can quite safely assume that unlike in the Cold War, "mutually assured destruction" is not on the cards. But other kinds of damage certainly cannot be excluded.

The EU Commission, which started the procedure, takes the view that it has legality on its side, that the restructuring of the administration of the law in Poland is so far-reaching as to destroy the autonomy of the rule of law. The Polish government says no. What is happening is the removal of judges who were a part of the communist power apparatus and, therefore, seen as incapable of rendering objective judgements. These two positions are irreconcilable, whether by legal or by political criteria. The net result is that political assessments have acquired primacy. This is bad for legality, of course, because seemingly legal decisions are perceived as driven by political interest.

Whether the EU has the legal right to take this step is itself hazy. It's an open question whether there has been a corresponding "conferral of power" by member states to the EU, as laid down in Article 4 of the Treaty (TEU). This is quite unclear. However, what is clear is that if the member state believes that the Commission's move is not justified legally, it can appeal against it to the EU Court. Once again, the legal and the political are confused. Still, the central question at issue is whether the EU is a single legal space. If so, then the Commission should be treating all member states even-handedly. This is manifestly not the case. There are serious dysfunctions in the administration of the law in more than one member state.

A few examples will suffice. In Slovakia, the Constitutional Court is barely functional, there are only 10 justices in office out of 13. There has been a several year-long dispute over the appointment of new members of the Court. The government nominates, the President approves, except that the President refused to accept the government's nominees, on the ground that these were politically grounded, in other words that the said nominees were political placemen (and women). In the Czech Republic (a.k.a. Czechia), there's a long running turf war between the Constitutional Court and the Supreme Court, with the latter ignoring decisions of the former. Something similar happens in Slovenia and Spain. But the EU Commission takes no interest in these parallel cases; indeed, in conversation Frans Timmermans, then first vice-president of the EU Commission, as good as admitted that the EU lacks the capacity to monitor the ruler of law in all the member states. That immediately raises the question of a double standard. And there is nothing like inconsistency to undermine credibility.

Hence we are back to politics, to the political background of why Poland has been singled out. In brief, the elections of 2015 brought to power the national-conservative PiS government that has repeatedly outraged left-liberal opinion, basically by seeking to eliminate the remnants of the communist regime. Note that these remnants have retooled themselves as liberals and democratic socialists, a metamorphosis that the West accepted without further question. Note another double standard here. The remnants of the Nazi German system were not so accepted and when East Germany reunited with the West, there was a very extensive purge of the selfsame communist remnants.

Poland, on the other hand, may not do likewise and the question is, why? In short, it's the defence of liberalism as currently understood and practised in the EU. This liberalism has never really taken root in Central Europe, not least because in a way it was kidnapped by the former communist power elite through a sophisticated salvaging operation during the shift from communism to democracy. Hence in Central Europe the liberal worldview of the West has been restricted to, at best, maybe ten percent of the population, mostly in the capital cities. The 2018 presidential elections in the Czech Republic demonstrated this very clearly. The candidate favoured by the left, Drahoš, won about two-thirds of the vote in Prague; Zeman, written off as a right-wing populist, won with the support of the countryside. Capital cities can no longer dominate the country, as they once used to be able to. In the local elections in Poland in 2018, specifically in Warsaw, the Platforma candidate Rafał Trzazkowski, won the first round with 54 percent; the countryside voted conservative. In the European Parliamentary elections in Hungary in 2019, in Budapest Fidesz received just over two-fifths of the vote. The situation in Slovakia, Slovenia and Serbia is analogous. All this suggests that the capital-countryside divide has come to create a new asymmetry, with political consequences.

At this point, our intrepid interstellar traveller should become aware of a significantly bigger gap between the EU-14[1] and the EU-11, always assuming that he has the cultural and political acuity to see this. The relationship between the Western and Central areas of Europe is set apart not only by the 45 year long communist period, but by much else.

So there is something else here. Central Europe, indeed all the former communist states, differ from those in the West, sometimes markedly, given their very different histories. This is the other Europe. It is, indeed, European, but not in the way in which being European is currently defined in Paris or Berlin or Brussels. The broad historical panorama, and its consequences, can be summarised as the problem of repeated transformations imposed on the region and resistance.

What gives the region this own shared affinity is a set of experiences, not shared identically, but close enough. In brief, for centuries the region has been exposed to external cultural, political, economic, social and other influences, over which they never had full control, but which impacted on them nevertheless. Some of these influences were cultural imports intended to strengthen local power. Others were imposed by external powers. The outcome of these processes was incompleteness, the cultural, political, other imports never quite worked as they had done in their countries of origin. Take feudalism, for example. This worked reasonably well as a system of administering land and establishing a hierarchy of control by royal power in the case of France, say. Compare that to Poland where feudal – indeed, late feudal – potentates established themselves as de facto autonomous rulers.

Or, think of the Baroque, the style of the Counter-Reformation. In its original iteration, it sought to promote the greater glory of God by incorporating the world into a single complex – have a look at any Baroque altar to see what I mean. I have particular affection for the high altar at the Abbey of Melk. But equally, the Counter-Reformation imposed its

---

[1]   I will refer to the pre-2004 member states as the EU-14, aware that this is a multiple anachronism, but at the time of writing the UK was only legally a member of the EU, no longer so politically. The term EU-11 refers to the enlargements of 2004, 2007 and 2011.

version of Catholicism on a region that was imbued by Protestantism, so the imposition took place by fire and sword. Think here of the execution of the Czech intelligentsia after the Battle of the White Mountain or the vicious torture used to put Protestants to death at the Bloody Assizes in Eperjes (Prešov). The result was, again, incompleteness, a project that had encountered resistance. This resistance does not fade away, typically the title given recently to a collection of writings by the great Hungarian writer Mihály Babits was "Be Resistance" (2008).

So, the central experience of the nations of the region was the loss of collective agency or the regaining of this agency only to have it diluted again. Empires were superimposed local political communities or equally on pre-political peasantry. The legacy of these empires and the resistance to them lives on. What is indisputable, however, is that empire and democracy (defined as the consent of the governed) are irreconcilable and imperial elites are answerable to no one. A democratic empire is akin to hot ice.

What we have in common in the region, therefore, is a particular thought-style, a particular way of understanding and structuring ideas and problems. The legacy of the Baroque can be glimpsed in the emphasis we place on aesthetics. The legacy of the 19th century reception of nationhood and nationalism was and is an intense emotionality that has then to be offset by irony and scepticism. But above all, we have our sensitivity, a great sensitivity, to having our preferences disregarded. And in this context, both the West (Germany, Austria, France, Italy) and the East (Russia, Ottomans) have been in the forefront.

Think of all the schemes of social engineering that outside powers have imposed on the region. The simultaneous creation of mono-ethnic and multi-ethnic states after 1918, the latter run by one hegemonic national collectivity. These did not work well, to put it mildly. So, after 1945, the West and the Soviet Union oversaw a set of massive population transfers and promoted ethnic homogenisation. Today, the winds of fashion blow from another direction and we are upbraided for wanting to be mono-ethnic.

Ideally, the region should be allowed to decide for ourselves, but that's the ghost in the machine, that superior power will invariably seek to subordinate weaker power. That's been the fate of Central Europe for centuries and that's why we can justifiably be seen as former intra-European colonies. It hardly needs adding that former colonies, whether in Europe or elsewhere, will deplore external attempts to exercise power over what these countries see as their own affair. Central Europeans, are more than aware of this sensitivity. By and large, the West fails to understand this, former imperial powers to the east and south don't seem to care.

Before the 2004 enlargement of the EU, a set of criteria were formulated, in Copenhagen it so happens, hence called Copenhagen criteria. Basically, these are the propositions laid out in Article 2 of the Treaty, the basic values of EU membership. The fact that these criteria were formulated before the accession of the communist former states is not without relevance. There is more than an implication that the older member states, the EU-14, did not fully trust the newer members, eventually to be the EU-11. The central difficulty is that while legally their fully equal status was safeguarded by law, politically and culturally that equality, that parity of esteem has never been established. Hence the interpretation of the core values of the EU was not open to the EU-11, in a word there was a built-in inequality.

It is, of course, impossible to be certain of this, but it is no wild guess that when the Copenhagen criteria were formulated, no one thought that some in the accession states, some politicians would seek to interpret European values by their own lights or needs. There was an implicit assumption of the identity of the rules and of their interpretation. In the real world, matters are never so simple. Each and every system of rules is subject to constant reinterpretation, in order to bring them into conformity with the circumstances that change in time and space. Guessing further, it would never have occurred to the norms entrepreneurs of the EU-14 that the EU-11 would also demand equal rights in the interpretation of the Copenhagen criteria as an integral aspect of the parity of esteem and that these interpretations would not necessarily be the same as those of the EU-14.

Yet this is what has happened. The EU-11, given its multiple differences from the EU-14, has begun to insist on the validity of its own valorisation of what Europe is, what democracy is, what human rights are. For the EU-14 this is a malign attack on their monopoly of knowledge and value production. It only adds to the problem that the EU-14 (obviously not in equal measure) starts from an unacknowledged, but real all the same, cultural disdain for Central Europe. This is deeply encoded, it goes back to the 18th century, if not earlier. What it signifies in the present context is that values articulated by Central Europe simply need not be taken seriously because they are regarded as inherently dubious or divergent, if not actually inferior.

One example from my own experience should suffice. At a meeting (in 2017) with a mixed group of young EU journalists, from EU-14 mostly, I was asked if I was not "ashamed" of the Hungarian government's policy towards immigrants (they had the fence in mind). I said no, on the contrary. Hungary did not wish to be a multicultural country, this was a question of democratic choice. Some countries had, indeed, opted to be multicultural, others, like Hungary and the rest of Central Europe, had decided otherwise. There was a palpable sense of shock among the assembled journos. The proposition that multiculturalism was a matter of choice had not been a part of their cultural capital.

The dominant liberal elites of the West have never accepted or understood this, hence they are all too ready to see Central Europe as deviant. The narrative of "democratic backsliding" is accepted as "a truth universally acknowledged". Hence the proposition requires no proof. (I was present when Hillary Clinton pronounced these very words during a formal visit to Budapest in 2011, voicing a not too subtle disapproval of the Hungarian government. She offered no proof either.)

And the Western liberals have their counterparts in the region – they can reasonably be called comprador intellectuals who seek to transpose and not infrequently impose Western values to their home countries. One of the more extreme illustrations of this activity comes from Poland. The well-known liberal think tank, the Batory Foundation, the citadel of Polish liberalism, published a pamphlet in 2017 with the title, "A Normative Empire in Crisis". Just to complete the picture, the metaphor of empire in *statu nascendi* was used by the veteran German social democrat Wolfgang Streeck, albeit in a strongly negative fashion.

The title of the Batory document is in itself revealing, possibly more than the author intended, because it actually uses the word "empire" for European values, does so approvingly and de facto locates them in the EU-14; the compradors of the EU-14 are on the side of the angels, of course. As I have already suggested, I regard democracy and empire as incommensurable, but such are the habits of mind of the liberal elite, that imposing a normative empire on Poland (elsewhere by extension) is regarded as unassailably democratic. To my mind, this adds up to a decidedly odd kind of liberalism, one that is more than tainted by an elitist authoritarianism, in as much as it is comfortable with imposing values on society and, logically, policies derived from those values. If society holds values at odds with these imperial norms, then too bad for society. As the old Balkan proverb has it, "if the rock should fall on the egg, alas for the egg; if the egg should fall on the rock, alas for the egg".

The point is, of course, that the norms in question do have an excellent fit with the needs of the liberal elite, because they make the questioning of these norms not just superfluous but a challenge to the naturalised order. In sum, the report essentialises European values, tacitly insists that these are defined exclusively by the elite and that everyone else must perform kow-tow. The argument of the report has the air of being the ultimate, irrevocable moral legislative account of the European identity. Thereby it excludes large swathes of society.

This liberalism has come a long way from its forefathers – Mill and Tocqueville – and sees itself currently as the sole and exclusive arbiter of what is right and wrong in the world. It has its origins in Blair's Third Way, in the exit strategy of the left in Europe after the collapse of communism and in its triumph in the great culture wars.

The intellectual, and more strikingly the moral superiority that is claimed by this liberal elite can be better understood in the context of the series of historic victories that it has achieved – over religion (no longer "exemplary and binding"), over fascism, communism, conservatism (including Christian Democracy) and over nationhood, especially anything that resembles ethnic solidarity. Seen in this light, its hubris becomes understandable, but nemesis has begun to emerge. In effect, liberalism claims a hegemony over democracy and does its best suppress anything that might challenge this.

Here an argument that liberalism is in the grip of a historicism, believes itself to have been sent by history to change the world, is very cogent. Indeed, one can take the reasoning further, to the effect that liberalism (in its current iteration) is increasingly moved by a narrative of election, not that of a people chosen by God but by "History" itself. The much repeated trope of being "on the wrong side of history" is evidence. But does history really have sides? Does it have an inside and outside? A top and a bottom? Beware of metaphors, don't be seduced by them! The real danger of relying on "History" to legitimate one's narratives is that it is a temptation to see the world as driven by "historical inevitability" and expose oneself to the moral monism that Isaiah Berlin warned against so eloquently.

This liberal hegemony, to use Gramsci's word, has a solid sociological basis. With local variations in Europe, Western Europe primarily, it has the support of around a quarter to a third of the population. They are the mobile beneficiaries of globalisation, the products of higher education and increasingly they are establishing themselves as a hereditary class, given assortative mating, the tendency to marry within the class, and to transmit their status to the next generation. The slowing down of upward social mobility and the rise of status inequality are the concomitants. Large swathes of the population have not only been living with real wage stagnation, but even more painfully, with loss of status (to quote her again, these are Hillary's "deplorables"). Not surprisingly the latter are beginning to demonstrate their dislike of these losses. This is the nemesis moment noted in the foregoing.

The rise of new political movements, disdained by the liberals as "populists", "xenophobes", "nativists", "racists" and the like, is likely to be a permanent phenomenon; liberalism seems to have peaked and to have generated an opposition that does not buy the liberal package and with which the liberals cannot cope. This helps to explain why liberalism relies on technocratic solutions, outsourcing politics to the judiciary, NGOs, lobbies, advocacy groups – anything that keeps the voters away from political decision-making. Hence the excoriation of the Brexit vote, of the election of Trump and, in a somewhat lower key, the denunciation of the Hungarian government's referenda and national consultations (disclosure: I have been a Fidesz MEP, so you may think I'm not in accord with the liberal hegemony, yes, admitted freely).

How the EU comes into this is a separate, but interlinked story. The Commission is formally "the guardian of the Treaties", a guardianship that implies – or should – a degree of ideological neutrality. In reality, this neutrality is rather weak now, because the Commission has overwhelmingly accepted the liberal package and understands Europe as a liberal Europe, despite the slogan of unity in diversity; the latter increasingly exists in rhetorical terms only. Historically this shift is interesting, because the origins of European integration are unequivocally Christian Democrat, but that, as the Americans say, is history.

There are several inferences to be drawn from this proposition. First, the integration process is near exclusively seen as a liberal project, which necessarily means that non-liberals are painted into the Eurosceptic corner. Any questioning of what the EU does is, therefore, automatically deemed both Eurosceptic and populist. Second, the supporters of a federal Europe have come to regard the Commission as their key redoubt, as their stronghold against the populist tide, which then moves them yet further towards technocracy and the exclusion, to the extent that it's feasible, of the voters. For them, the idea of a demos-free democracy is more than a pipedream. There is an intriguing thought-experiment here: can there be a democracy without a demos? And, third, liberalism seems committed to yet another social engineering project, that of converting all or most of the population of Europe into European federalists (or else). Dream on.

This brings us back to Poland and the liberals' determination to bring the PiS government into line. There is no sign of this actually happening, indeed precisely because the confrontation has gone so far, neither it nor the Commission can retreat. It goes without saying that in any dispute this is a dangerous situation. The Commission has de facto become an actor in Polish domestic politics and whether it has either the legal right or the political legitimacy to do so is very much open to doubt.

If the great clash between Central Europe and the liberals of the West – or maybe they should be called liberal Jacobins – were restricted to questions of normativity, then this could be seen as a teething problem of European integration that would eventually fade away, as the EU-11 acquired parity of esteem. The problem is that structural factors that manifestly disadvantage the EU-11 underlie the normativity problem. EU membership in the 1990s was legitimated by a number of arguments – from security advantages, from being inside a network, and above all by that of reaching the Western standard of living, the great dream of "catching up". This has not happened. Basically, not one of the former communist states has reached the level of the GDP per capita of the EU-14. Two exceptions do not affect this picture. Slovenia and the

Inflows vs outflows in Eastern Europe (% GDP, annual averages, 2010-2016)

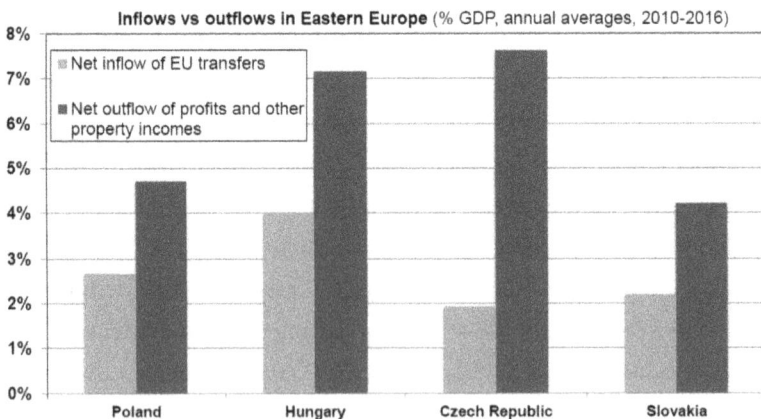

Source: author's computations using Eurostat national accounts and EU budget series.
Reading: between 2010 and 2016, the annual net transfers from the European Union (total expenditures received minus total contributions paid to EU budget) amounted to 2.7% of GDP per year on average in Poland; during the same period, the annual outflow of profits and other property incomes (net of corresponding inflow) amounted to 4.7% of GDP.

Czech Republic had a higher GDP per capita than Portugal and Greece on accession and still do. That's it. The dream of "catching up" remains that. It is impossible to escape the conclusion that EU's single market – the free movement of capital – has played role in this. Indeed, the figures produced by Thomas Piketty, whose leftwing and EU-14 credentials are impeccable, more than bears this out. In sum, capital outflows from Central Europe more than exceed capital arrivals, thereby making local capital accumulation that much more difficult.

Piketty adds the explanatory comment,

> Between 2010 and 2016, the annual outflow of profits and incomes from property (net of the corresponding inflows) thus represented on average 4.7% of the gross domestic product in Poland, 7.2% in Hungary, 7.6% in the Czech Republic and 4.2% in Slovakia, reducing commensurately the national income of these countries.

To Piketty's analysis, we can add that of another leftwing writer, Federico Fubini, an Italian journalist. His central concern is the impact of out-migration on those who stay and the benefits that the receiving countries acquire (for free). Migrants from Central Europe have basically compensated for Germany's demographic decline – Germany has registered more annual deaths than births since 1972. Furthermore, argues Fubini, these rather poorer Central European states have transmitted around €100 million to the wealthier West through the investment in the migrants' education and training. This, he suggests, is a kind of invisible transfer union, in which the poor subsidise the rich. Besides, those who go are often the most energetic and innovative, in consequence of which there are productivity losses in the sending states, a factor that helps to explain their inability to catch up.

So, Fubini writes, "By 2016, the annual income of Western Europe (the average of Germany, France, the UK, Italy, the Netherlands, Belgium, Sweden, and Finland) was 42% above that of [the average of Estonia, Poland, Hungary and Romania] compared to 60% above in 1989.

Yet in cash terms, the average annual income gap (all data are in 2011 dollars, adjusted for purchasing power) was $14,751 in 1989 and had grown to just $17,647 by 2016." This is a staggering gap, it places a major question mark over the EU's vaunted four freedoms, it challenges free marketeers in their belief (and it is no more than that) that an equilibrium will work its way through. And it underscores the asymmetry of economic, and thereby political power, between Central Europe and the West. We should not be surprised at the resentment in the former. No one likes to discover that whatever they do, however hard they work, however much they improve their productivity, they will still be on the periphery.

Another perspective on this centre-periphery issue is known beguilingly as the blue banana proposition, *banane bleu* to be precise, because it was coined by the French activist Jacques Chérèque and developed by the similarly French geographer, Roger Brunet. Their thesis is that there is an urban megalopolis stretching from Manchester to Milan, resembling the shape of a banana, and this is where the concentration of technology, innovation and networks are to be found. Central Europe is conspicuously absent. The 15 years of EU membership have done nothing to change this. Evidently, capital poverty and demographic losses have much to do with this state of affairs, even if the causation is murky.

The inference is clear enough. EU membership has not brought the desired economic advantage to Central Europe and that has political and cultural implications, not just economic ones. It raises at sensitive question over the role of the Commission. If the Commission is supposed to be the neutral guardian of the treaties, is it in any way entrusted with a role of establishing a degree of fairness in the way in which the capital markets work, evidently to the disadvantage of Central Europe? The Commission is silent on this, but that earns it the distrust of growing numbers of people in the region.

The stand-off is beginning to resemble a frozen conflict. We are familiar enough with these outside Europe, but if we look without blinkers, there is a seepage. Divided Cyprus has been around for so long that it's below the radar. Independent Kosovo is not recognised by five EU member states. Brexit has thrown up the problem of the intractable border between Northern Ireland and the Irish Republic, as well as the status of Gibraltar. The crisis in Catalonia is far from resolved. The opposition to migrant quotas remains in being. The frontier dispute between Slovenia and Croatia has just reached the agenda of the EU and the future of the Eurozone is still open. In these circumstances, adding the conflict with Poland seems like a luxury.

That may well be an understatement. The European integration process was initiated after 1945 to act as a conflict resolution mechanism, above all to ensure that there would never be another war between France and Germany. This has been brilliantly successful. Others can be added, like the Good Friday agreement that settled the Troubles in Northern Ireland. From this perspective, putting the conflict with Poland agenda seems counter-productive if not bizarre. Could a political solution have been found between the Commission and the Polish government? Given the EU's track record, it's hard to say no.

In this connection, think of the 2019 European Parliamentary elections. The slogans of "who rules?" and "take back control" are ready to be deployed and, who knows, the European Parliament could find itself with a blocking minority of Eurosceptics, which will make EU legislation difficult, to say the least.[2]

Finally, a hypothetical – suppose that somehow the Commission is successful and Poland is actually deprived of its voting rights. But a member state of the EU also has a nuclear option. The Polish government could call early elections and win on a "who rules?" basis, possibly with a constitutional majority. What then? What is the EU's exit strategy? Can the integration process cope? How will the other 27 member states respond? If the Austrian boycott of 2000 is a precedent, they will be decidedly uneasy. Still, my hypothetical is unlikely to reach that state of affairs.

---

2 The jury is still out on this at the time of writing, mid-June 2019. The Eurocritical forces performed better than before, but did not attain a majority. Whether they can mobilise blocking minorities remains to be seen.

All the same, beware of the unintended consequences of your actions, not to mention of what you wish for. Scenarios, however well plotted, never quite turn out as you would like them. Kant's crooked timber comes to mind all too readily.

References

Fubini, Federico. 2019. "The Roots of European Division", *Project Syndicate*, 17 May 2019 https://www.project-syndicate.org/onpoint/the-roots-of-european-division-by-federico-fubini-2019-05. Accessed 20 May 2019.

Piketty, Thomas. 2018. L'année de l'Europe, *Le Monde blog* 16 January 2018, http://piketty.blog.lemonde.fr/2018/01/16/2018-the-year-of-europe. Accessed 17 January 2018.

Streeck, Wolfgang. 2019. "The EU is a doomed empire", *Le Monde Diplomatique*, 19 May 2019 https://mondediplo.com/2019/05/06eu. Accessed 21 May 2019.

Interview (transcription) appeared in geopolitica.ru, the interviewer was Sofia Metelkina

In your opinion, what is the biggest lie of liberalism?

The biggest lie?

Or the biggest illusion of liberalism.

Illusion and lie are not the same thing. I mean a lie is a conscious, deliberate falsehood. An illusion may be a misunderstanding, an error in perception. My experience with the liberals I encounter is that they are firmly convinced that what they say is right. They have an illusion. They have a fallacy. But I think that in grand intellectual, historical terms, what has happened is that classical liberalism has been transformed, from that of Tocqueville, John Stuart Mill...or Francis Lieber, a German-American, who wrote in the second half of the nineteenth century. He was a contemporary of Tocqueville's. I don't think they ever met. Their starting point was that the individual has certain inalienable rights. We can, by the way, trace that back to Christianity. You can find various roots. And I think this has now been magnified to such an extent – distorted, if you like – that there are only rights, and there is only the individual. And my argument is that, as individuals, if we do not have some collective identity, we're lost. We lose our humanity. Now, what that collective identity is, well, there is an infinite variety. It can be a trade union. It can be a regiment. It can be a school. It can also be a nation. Civilization? I don't really know what a civilization is, but we can argue about it.

So then the question is to what extent does that collective identity determine the individual's worldview? And I think that it does, but it still, depending on the identity we're talking about, leaves quite a lot of autonomy for the individual. But I think what has happened is that the current iteration of liberalism denies all collective identity, or comes very close to it, because it believes in a single, universal humanity. Well, very nice. Yes, I think there are a few qualities that all human beings have. Basically, we all have two lungs and one heart, but the moment you reduce humanity to a single entity, you eliminate cultural variation. You are unable to understand quite a wide range of phenomena which you then condemn. "It's deviant, wrong, morally unacceptable," and so on and so forth.

To me, I think this is the flaw, the error of liberalism, which I think today – it wasn't necessarily so twenty years ago – has become linked to a utopianism and has become linked to a sense of mission, that liberals are sent by themselves, or history or humanity, or whoever, to save the world.

Now, I'm sure you're familiar with salvationism. Soteriology is the technical term. I do see this – not obviously in every liberal, but they have a very, very strong belief in their own correctness which may not be questioned. At that point, I think one has departed from what I understand to be the liberal tradition: that you remain open to dialogue, you remain open to discourse, because if you don't, then you generate a frustration in your interlocutor. And that frustration can result in pretty negative consequences. Indeed violence, in certain circumstances. You know, when you have social tensions accumulating, and there's no other way of resolving them, you may get an explosion, of which there are countless examples in history.

What will happen to humanity in the liberal paradigm when we see the eternal division in everything, the reign of quantity. Many of us are losing collective identity. Even the individual has become like a jigsaw puzzle, where you can replace his hand, or maybe eventually even his brain, with electronics. It's the old philosophical problem of division, so what do you see . . .

Which division do you have in mind?

I mean the principle of division.

I think I see what you mean. Binary opposition?

Also. For example, we had people, identities, big families. Now we see that in big cities there are individuals, individualism like a principle, and it is an example of this division. And even one person is sometimes no longer complete.

So this is the divided humanity.

Yes.

Well, I think that that is our legacy. I think that you can't, in my view, find wholeness. You can try to be holistic, but you can never reach it, because it's our basic heritage that there will always be divisions and contradictions and dissonances in what we are and what we do, how we respond to different situations, and I don't want to get too biological, but I think that in certain circumstances biology plays a role: I don't know, whatever you've eaten. Did you have a good lunch? If you had a good lunch, you feel better, etcetera, etcetera. In a word, the contingency of life. So I'm simply saying that it's the infinite diversity, the infinite variety of possible responses, and that kind of division will always exist. The role of the ruler, of society I think is to establish some kind of order, otherwise there's chaos, some kind of stability, and perhaps just as much as anything else predictability. Broadly speaking, you can evolve a strategy, which may change over time, that, on the whole, things will be much the same tomorrow as they are today. If that is upset, if you have arbitrary action which transforms the predictability, then I think you get a lot of negative consequences.

What do you think of the idea of illiberalism?

The term illiberalism is, of course, not mine. The term illiberalism was propounded by the Hungarian Prime Minister, Viktor Orbán. Note that, to the best of my knowledge, he only ever used that word a few times, I think several years ago (in 2014). It has acquired a set of meanings which have been attributed to that word, and indeed to Orbán, by outsiders. What I see as illiberalism, which may not correspond to anybody else's view, is a questioning of extreme individualism, the questioning of inequalities. I'm not a radical egalitarian. There will always be differences. But I think that the levels of material, and also cognitive, inequality in the world are, for me, morally unacceptable. Not just between, let's say, the rich West and Africa, but within European states.

There is a very interesting French social geographer, Christophe Guilluy. He basically argues that centre-periphery has come into being within France, and I think one can apply that insight to pretty much every European state. Probably Russia, too. Actually, if I think about it, I suspect that certain parts remote from the centres are pretty marginal. Or the Western country that I know best, which is Britain. I'm sure you've been to London. Glittering world city, everything, and then if you travel north, to northern England, you see a very, very different country. Not material poverty, but intellectual poverty, cognitive poverty. Meaningless lives. And it's that kind of inequality that concerns me, which I think is a consequence of the proposition that markets solve everything. I think the State does have a role. Where that role is, where is the dividing line between State and market, it's always going to be a matter of argument.

What we had in Hungary, and this is where the Hungarian version of illiberalism comes in, is that we had a leftwing government from 2002 to 2010 which pursued extreme market liberal policies, the consequence of which was close to bankruptcy for the State. Very close. Almost. When the Fidesz government was elected in 2010, it discovered that the deficit left behind – I've forgotten the exact figure – was far greater than what anybody understood, the net result of which set the country very close to the kind of bankruptcy – collapse – that Greece entered. So basically, Orbán took a decision – you know, each European Union country has to maintain its deficit within three percent – he went to Brussels and said to Barroso, "We've inherited this problem. Can we have some easing on the three percent?" And Barroso said, "No." So at that point Orbán understood that Brussels, the Commission, was not going to be very well-disposed towards his government. What they really wanted him to do was to introduce an austerity policy which, in a relatively poor country like Hungary (this is no longer quite so acute), would hit the most marginal very hard. It was already tricky. It's not so true now, but in some parts of Hungary there were children who basically had next to nothing to eat from Friday until Monday because their parents couldn't afford very much to eat, so they'd only eat at school. This is appalling. In my humble opinion, I think this is intolerable in a moderately well-to-do, medium-sized European state.

So there was no way that the Fidesz government was going to accept a restrictive policy that would hit those marginal sectors of society, strata, even harder. So, the government introduced a so-called unorthodox policy of taxing internationals, taxing banks, taxing telecoms, multinationals, thanks to which the worst was avoided. This was extremely unpopular in Brussels because it went against the conventional liberal orthodoxy, which, at least in my view, has captured Brussels. It is unable to think in different terms, and from that perspective, Hungary became deviant. Nobody likes deviants. Deviants have to be brought back into the "liberal" fold.

So when Orbán made this speech at Tușnad, he said, "What we're building here is an illiberal state. Of course, we maintain all the classical freedoms." Now, that's the bit that everybody forgets. That speech has to be studied very closely. The illiberalism that Orbán was talking about is basically a form of etatism, that the State has a role to play in social protectionism. And by the way, this is not that far from either Christian democracy or social democracy, but liberalism has done something else, very interesting in grand historical terms: it has established a monopoly over democracy. If you're a democrat, you're going to be a liberal democrat. I don't accept this position. I think there are all sorts of different forms of democracy. And in that sense, Orbán's illiberal perspective is well within the confines of democracy.

Now for me – because I think this begs the question of what I mean by democracy – it is a system of power where rule is by the consent of the governed, and that there is a degree of institutional pluralism. What degree? Well, we'll argue about that. Rule of law, checks-and-balances, sure, etcetera. So that's how I would define illiberalism. It's not an absolute concept, to some extent it's fluid, what you accept as being within it, what you accept as outside of it. But I would add again that this is not the way in which it is used by much of the Western media. For them, illiberalism is very close to the devil. It has acquired a demonic content that almost seems to have become a semiotic code. You say the word "illiberal" and you automatically associate it with otherwise undefined phenomena. Very, very interesting. It has even got a strong metaphorical charge, which means you can't deconstruct the word "illiberal" because it'll not be heard, because it's already so strongly established that it excludes alternative definitions and meanings. I think you will recognize this as being very close to Bakhtin's monology.

What are the factors that make Fidesz popular?

First of all, the economy is doing quite well. I'm not a Marxist, I'm not a materialist, but I have to accept that, yes, the fact that the economy is doing well in some sectors – there is even a labour shortage in skilled manual labour, mostly – we have been going up slowly, but still well behind Germany, or Austria for that matter. But still, there's an improvement, and it's palpable. And there's been quite an impressive visual change in infrastructure – it's not all there, and the railways are still not very good, but still. The motorways are not doing too badly. Support for the family is one of the best in Europe. Health has taken a lot of cuts. Not good. And what sits close to my heart, of course, is education. Education is always the easiest target for a government that wants to cut spending, and that's always easy to do. In those two areas especially, considerable monies will have to be spent in time to come.

Then, I think the stand that the government took in 2015 on migration has been of central significance. Now, I don't know if you've seen the pictures – because I'm sure you weren't in Budapest in the summer of 2015 – these unbelievable pictures of the Eastern railway station, of the Keleti . . . It was a form of structural violence. Basically, it's unimaginable to me that two hundred thousand plus – maybe more, I'm not sure how many people – just simply walk through Hungary as if it didn't exist. A country which cannot control its frontiers, which cannot control who comes into that country and who does not, unless there's a derogation like Schengen, is not a proper country in the Weberian sense, because I think it is a part of the monopoly of legitimate violence for a State to be able to say, "You can come in and you cannot." Now, this having deeply shocked Hungarian opinion, certainly the people I spoke to – well, I think I can fairly say I was shocked myself – it's pretty shocking to see a scene that is fairly familiar to you suddenly transformed in a way that is beyond the control of the State.

So I think that that general experience, it was traumatic for quite a lot of people, because they'd had no idea, they'd never had experience of this number of people. I mean, Budapest is already very different from what it was fifty years ago. Obviously tourists started coming. Fine. But that was something completely different. And I think the fact that the government as such took a very strong stand on migration, built the fence, and said, "No, you can't come in here just like that" . . . And this again was distorted in the Western media. They depicted the fence as something to stop people from coming in. No! The fence was there to ensure that people went to the frontier crossing point where they could be registered. And registration takes time, so there's no way that one could register two thousand people a day. Some people got stuck on the Serbian side, or they went off to Croatia, but gradually, over time, I think much of European opinion has come to accept that Europe can't absorb this number of migrants. Hungary has, to the best of my knowledge, not accepted any migrants, we've accepted refugees. That's a distinction that I think is well worth making. The Geneva Convention: if you're in fear for your life for political reasons, or you come from a war zone, that sort of thing, then of course you will be given political asylum, refugee status. If you're an economic migrant, then Hungary doesn't need economic migrants.

And then of course you get into the whole problem of the dispute between Hungary and Germany over *Willkommenskultur*, over Merkel saying, "Let everybody come," but – come through Hungary? Excuse me? Merkel basically imposed *Willkommenskultur* on Europe, without Europe's consent. Certainly without Hungary's consent. So that friction, that tension, remains of course . . . In Europe today, Germany is a pre-eminent partner – I say partner, because we're in a partnership – but we do have disputes, and that's one of them. I think also that Hungary, you have to understand, is a deeply conservative country. Conservative not in the political sense necessarily, but in a cultural-sociological sense. To give you one illustration, in terms of music, I think this country is still in the 1930s. Contemporary music simply has no reception. People haven't learned the language of Stockhausen. You may not like Stockhausen, but you still have to accept that he's one of the major figures in European musical terms. I think one of the great composers of the twentieth century is Villa Lobos. Unknown in Hungary. In that sense, culturally, there is a great deal of conservatism, reluctance to accept the new. You can trace this back to a series of repeated traumas. Now, you may be familiar with cultural trauma theory. After such traumas, society becomes defensive and introverted, and tries to save what it can.

I'm not going to take you through the twentieth-century history of Hungary, but before 1914, this was a very self-satisfied and successful society. Look around Budapest today. This building where we are, the Gresh-

am Palace, was built in, I think, 1906. It's been beautifully restored. I like
it very much. And there was enormous self-confidence about building a
really major European city, which I think was quite successful. Then you
have this series of shocks, traumas, and changes viewed very negatively:
the Second World War, 1956, to some degree even the system change in
1989, and this sense that things are happening to us without our ability
to affect them, to influence them, even to change them. It's in that sense
that this is a conservative society. And one of the things that I believe
Orbán, and indeed the Fidesz government, is trying to do is to change
this, to give Hungarian society self-confidence – it's happening slowly –
and at the same time, to define a particular Hungarian version of modernity. What does it mean to be modern and Hungarian?

Now, the liberals will tell you there is only one modernity. This is not
true. It's simply not true on the evidence. Have you ever been to Japan?

No.

Well, basically, Japan is modern, but it's very differently modern from
Germany or France or Britain, and it's in that sense that there are multiple modernities. This thought is anathema to a universalist. And that's
why, of course, for me illiberalism conveys this idea of the Hungarian
road to modernity. If you want to use the Marxist-Leninist terminology,
it's a polycentric modernity. Think about the 1960s. So it's in that sense
that I would define illiberalism, not in the sense in which the various or-
gans of the Western media try to do it.

*That's a very interesting explanation. I also have a question related to
your article, about the politically segmented society and the possibility
of civil war. What precisely did you mean by it in relation to Hungary?*

Okay. Segmentation theory, I use this in a fairly classical sense, based
mainly on the work of Furnivall, who was writing about Burma, and I
think Indonesia, before the Second World War. He was a very interest-

ing figure. He was an anthropologist, and I think also a colonial civil servant. I don't remember exactly. And what he writes is that there are different ethno-social religious groups which lead their own lives, so you have a state in which state and society are not coterminous. You have different segments operating. This, of course, was also the Austro-Hungarian Empire. How do you deal with this if you want to have something like a citizenship, then have to do one of two things: you can try to suppress the segments, which then generally ends up with the most powerful segment suppressing the others. It's basically the Russian Empire before 1914. Think about Uvarov: autocracy, Orthodoxy, the Czar, and so on. And the smaller segments have to conform, have to adapt. One of the problems of being in a minority is that you never own the narrative. The narrative is always constructed by the majority, which means that if you have a segmented society, you will always have resentment. Probably *ressentiment* is a better word for that: a deep feeling of not being central against the problem of agency.

What I see in Hungary – and I don't like it, but that is, I think, the sociological reality – is the existence of probably three segments. Maybe four, possibly five. It depends on how you define them. Politically, the divide between Left and Right is very, very deep. Fascinating – there is a hereditary transmission of segmental identity, so if you are born to a rightwing family, the chances are very high that you, too, will be rightwing, and vice versa. To some degree – not purely, it's not a one hundred percent overlap – the Right are the descendants of the victims of Communism, the Left are the legatees of the nomenklatura, the beneficiaries of Communism. And Communism did have its beneficiaries, let's be quite clear on this. So that's two segments.

The third segment is the radical Right, which we will see . . . Well, first of all, Jobbik is no longer quite as radical Right as it once was, it's trying to move in towards the centre, with what degree of sincerity I've no idea. What I can say about Jobbik is that they were pretty amateurish ten years ago. This is no longer true. They're quite professional, and they're all very good at using social media. They, too, have a vision of modernity. I think there is a very hard radical Right in Hungary, sort of seven to eight percent, and then the other bulk of Jobbik . . . Difficult to say, but in 2010 and 2014, much of the disaffected – very often underemployed or unemployed blue-collar strata – shifted from voting for the Left to voting for Jobbik. They don't shift to Fidesz, they shift to Jobbik because they are radical. This isn't well understood. If you're radical, you don't care whether you're radical Left or radical Right. You're radical. There are lots of historical examples. It's the radicalism that moves you. So that, I think, is one segment.

And indeed, if you want to break down the support for Jobbik, you find support in the rust belt of the northeast – in Miskolc, around there. Some of them in Budapest. There's a very interesting stratum of radical university students, almost all male, students who are anti-globalization. That, I think, is not just a Hungarian phenomenon. And then you have a very interesting phenomenon: the inroads that Jobbik has made in some of the smaller villages, especially in Transdanubia, who don't starve, but they don't have the opportunities which you get in the larger towns. So they're resentful, and Jobbik has been able to pick up their vote. Whether they'll get the fifteen percent or so on 8 April (the date of the parliamentary elections), I don't know.[1] They will probably do quite well. So that's my third segment.

I think a fourth segment is the Roma, probably a fifth segment being the third-largest Jewish community in Europe, which is overwhelmingly a Budapest community. They have a sense of separateness – to what degree or what extent is another matter.

So if you look at this, how do you then establish a citizenship which is acceptable to, let's say, ninety-five percent of the population? Probably, the Jobbik segment will accept most of the nationhood, though Fidesz is not radical enough for them. The Left will never accept that. The Left, I think, still denies the constitution, the basic law. They say that, "We want to change it." Well, that's politics. I think the Roma are reasonably

---

1   Jobbik received 19.06 percent of the votes at the 2018 parliamentary elections.

content with the ideas of national citizenship. Nationhood, I don't know. Some of them do feel they're Hungarian, some of them think they're Roma. It's probably a mixture.

But then you get this problem of what does citizenship and modernity mean, and indeed liberalism and the role of the State, if you're in one of the segments that is not the Fidesz segment? Well, you have to adapt, you have to adjust. Majoritarianism doesn't work perfectly because there will be, as I said, those who reject the majority position, particularly with the leftwing segment that is different. I don't think in Hungary anybody thinks about power-sharing or consociational solutions such as you used to have in the Netherlands and you still have in Belgium, Austria to some degree, and lots of examples from before the First World War.

In Moravia, the population was sixty percent Czech and forty percent German, or sixty-five, thirty-five, and in 1905 they came to a power-sharing agreement which would ensure that both parties were proportionately represented in political power so that ethnic identity, language, was no longer a central issue in the political contest.

In Estonia in the interwar period they introduced a similar arrangement, that the Germans, the Russians, Jews, the Swedes – these were the four minorities – would all establish corporations and be responsible for their own educational and cultural life and they would tax their members. They would, of course, accept Estonian citizenship and the Estonian state. The German corporation worked reasonably well. The Russians never got round to setting it up because they kept arguing. Remember that in Estonia there were two groups of Russians: the urban Russians of Tallinn and Narva at that time, and then the Old Believers. There was a community of about ten, twelve thousand Old Believers at Lake Peipus, and they never managed to get this together. The Jews were about to do it when the war broke out. The Swedes, very few in number, they were territorially compact, so they didn't need it. But the system worked adequately. Not perfect, but nothing is perfect. If Estonia had not been absorbed by the Soviet Union in 1940, then, of course, that experiment would have been continued.

So, that kind of power-sharing agreement can work. It requires the majority to accept that it can only run the country properly or adequately or sufficiently if it has the consent of the minority. That's what a system of that kind does in terms of segmentation.

I would like to ask you about the Russian-Hungarian, or rather Hungarian-Russian, relationship...

They're not the same. Hungarian-Russian and Russian-Hungarian are not the same, but both are significant.

We see that between Hungary and Poland there is diplomatic cooperation, and between Hungary and Russia there is cooperation, but between Poland and Russia there are big problems. First, will Russia be a problem in the relations among the countries of the Visegrád Group, and second, how do you see the relationship between Hungary and Russia?

On the Visegrád point, it obviously creates a certain amount of friction between Hungary and Poland, but then there is so much else which brings the V4 countries together that the two countries, I think, have agreed to disagree. Broadly, Hungary accepts the "Three Seas" idea. And there's a second point that ties in with the second part of your question. Hungary is very largely dependent on Russian energy. Poland is not. If we had a sea coast, it would be different. We'd be able to import liquefied natural gas on the global market. The pipelines are actually now an outdated technology compared to the LNG.

The problem is that about eighty-five percent of Hungarian energy, overwhelmingly gas, comes from Russia. So we have this transactional relationship with Russia where, whatever we do, we're dependent on Russian gas. I would add that both the United States and the European Union have been very slow in recognizing this kind of dependence. They've been much faster in recognizing the particular problem in Lithuania. Lithuania, for a long time, was an energy island. It isn't anymore. They've linked their power grid across the sea border with Sweden, and they have this LNG terminal in Klaipeda. So it's transformed Lithuania's dependence. Of course, Lithuania still buys gas from Russia. There's an LNG terminal being built in Finland, and there is one in Poland, in Świnoujście. The problem is the interconnectors to Hungary are not there, and actually, Gazprom has done everything to stop it.

The other possibility is an LNG terminal in Croatia, and the Croats have been very, very slow in doing anything. Since I first heard about this in 2007, that there was going to be an LNG terminal on the island of Krk – nothing. Slowly, under the present Croatian government, they're beginning to do something, and my understanding is that Hungary at one point asked Washington, "Could you help? Could you persuade the Croats to start building this?" And the Americans said, "But why? You're buying this gas from Russia." And we said, "We don't want to be too dependent." "Don't be paranoid. It's a commercial transaction." Well, it never was. From the 1990s already, Russia was talking about the "energy weapon." But the Americans never understood this.

So we're left in this situation of being energy dependent on Russia. Fine. Acceptable. It didn't raise eyebrows. And then came Crimea, and at that point the political context completely changed. So, Hungary's relationship with Russia became objectionable. Interestingly enough, Austria's relations with Russia is never questioned. Germany, determined to build Nord Stream 2: no. Hungary: yes. I'm neutral on nuclear power. I don't have a strong position on it. Rosatom offered to extend Paks, and the Orbán government considered it. The terms were very good. I'm not sure that Rosatom really has the money for this, but we'll see. Rosatom is very ambitious, building nuclear power stations everywhere. We'll see. The terms were very advantageous, and on top of that, there is a strong technological argument in enlarging Paks with Russian technology. It will cut costs in all sorts of areas if you use the same technology that you have already. I know that Westinghouse also offered, and apparently the terms were much worse, and they said, "We will enlarge Paks." And the

Hungarian government said, "This is an absolute impossibility. American nuclear technology and Russian nuclear technology simply won't mix." And Westinghouse was apparently very angry.

So in that sense, it's the energy area. Where I would say I'd like to see more investment now is in renewables, and there I think we're still very slow. We probably could be generating much more of our electrical power from renewables. There are some wind farms. Not many. I don't know how many in Hungary. More than there were ten years ago. Solar panels, much more remains to be done. The cost is dropping all the time. Chinese solar panels are very cheap now, and as you probably know, it's not the heat, it's the light that generates the energy.

I don't myself see any strong ideological overlap between Fidesz's position and Russia. Yes, Putin was here. He did go to the cemetery in Kerepesi út to lay a wreath at the memorial to the Red Army soldiers killed in 1956, and so on, which I think is a bit difficult for a Hungarian to swallow, because the Russians who were killed in 1956 were here as an invading force. They were not invited. But basically I think that, obviously, there will be individual exceptions. People who are involved in trade with Russia want to have maximally good relations, as you would expect, and they're opposed to the EU sanctions. Hungary has followed the EU sanctions, and I can't see any reason why that's a problem. There's a certain level of EU solidarity, and it was the Budapest Memorandum that Russia violated over Crimea. This has a certain sentimental resonance. That in exchange for Ukraine abandoning its nuclear armoury, Russia guaranteed the territorial integrity of Ukraine, only for so long.

So I don't myself see great depth in Hungary's relationship with Russia. From the other side, I think Hungary is completely marginal as far as Russia is concerned. You can use it to make trouble, but not more than that. There are much more important countries with which Russia has to deal. Germany, that's the most important EU country for Russia, not Hungary, and it's slightly absurd for Hungary to imagine that it is important. Where it becomes significant is if ever the European Union cohesion and structural funds dry up or diminish, then the opening to the East – Russia, Central Asia, China – can become significant as a source of investment. That's as far as I would take it, but you'll find others who take a different view of the Russian-Hungarian, Hungarian-Russian relationship. But that's my take on it.

What If?*

The European Parliament has decided, Hungary has been referred to Council under Article 7 of the TEU and the left is celebrating. We can leave to one side the questions over the voting procedure, given that politically the weight of the voting is what counts.

The joy unconfined on the left is understandable. After all, the left has long regarded Hungary as the seat of everything that it detests – it has devised a narrative that includes no rule of law, no judicial independence, no free media, no free anything really and presumably a nation of sheep who will vote for Fidesz because they are sheep. Quite some narrative. And those who contest it are automatically disregarded.

Pay no attention to the proposition that the evidence that Hungary has gone over to dark side is weak, indeed all too often absent. Ignore the fact, for fact it is, that the sources of the Western left's concerns frequently haven't a leg to stand on. They've been constructed by journalists who do not know enough Hungarian to buy a bar of soap, who seek out leftwing Hungarian sources – and only those – which are sincerely committed to blackening the government's name. So, when citing the work of a think-tank the foresaid journalists will never add that it's a leftwing body, not committed to purveying objective information. And then, there is the distinctive Hungarian habit of heaping exaggeration on hyperbole. Hungarians are used to this, but translate the sen-

---

*   Hungarian Review, Vol. IX, No.5, November 2018. http://www.hungarianreview.com/article/20181015_what_if.

timent into English or French, to an outsider it will sound like an end-time alert.

This is served up to Western readers in undiluted form because it makes great copy, except of course the Western readers can't know about the distorting mirror, about the tainted reporting, so they accept it as the unvarnished truth. It is far from exaggeration in this instance that it has become "a truth universally acknowledged" in the eyes of many that Hungary is an autocracy. All too often, such truths universally acknowledged are wholly erroneous, but that doesn't stop journalists from repeating them.

So forget about the Hungarian realities that are ignored by the media, like the hapless, fragmented political opposition which has still to work out what being leftwing means, apart from detesting Orbán. It was just a few years ago, that a senior adviser to the pre-2010 leftwing government was quoted to the effect that "the worst non-Orbán government is better than the best Orbán government". Not a lot of nuance there.

In the same way, ignore any evidence that is positive as far as the Fidesz government is concerned. The EU Commission's Justice Scoreboard is one of these, Hungary comes out not too badly at all, mostly in the top third of the 28. Some of what the Venice Commission has said about Hungary has been critical, but far from all, some of their findings has been supportive. Much the same can be said of the EU's Fundamental Rights Agency.

Well, of course, these must be ignored, because they get in the way of the narrative on the basis of which the 448 MEPs voted for the Sargentini report. What we have, then, is a well-established European value propagated by the left – a Manichean view in which the left attributes all virtue to itself and all vice to Fidesz, or to any other political movement that questions the bearers of light to the left.

If you add all these together, then the Sargentini report is a dystopic fabrication. Dystopic because it looked only for the worst (and found it) and fabrication because it ignored all the contrary evidence. Something wrong with the application of European values here, no?

The word "vice", used above, is not there by accident. The liberal hegemony has increasingly acquired many of the qualities of a secular belief system – unconsciously mimicking Christian antecedents – with a hierarchy of public and private evils. Accusations substitute for evidence, but one can scourge one's opponents (enemies, increasingly) by calling them racist or nativist or xenophobic. Maybe the Inquisition would be a better metaphor.

Absolute evil is attributed to the Holocaust, hence Holocaust denial and Holocaust banalisation are treated as irremediably sinful, even criminal in some countries. Clearly, the entire area is so strongly sacralised or tabooised that it is untouchable.

Not quite as far-reaching in the catalogue of evils is colonialism and slavery. Note by the way, that only European slavery counts. The many-centuries long Arab slave trade between east Africa and Araby is ignored. The pursuit of post-colonial guilt is arguably tied up with the presence of former colonial subjects in the metropole, as an instrument for silencing any voices that might be audacious enough to criticise Third World immigration.

Coming close to the foregoing in the catalogue and with intensifying emphasis is the condemnation of nationalism. Note a number of things here. First, the West has unilaterally declared itself post-national, though on what basis has never been made clear. It just sort of happened. Note too that in the real world this has not actually made the French less French or the Dutch less Dutch, but it's good to pretend otherwise. And, while we're at it, Brexit is unquestionably fuelled by a certain sense of injured Englishness.

Then, because one can't be a post-national without there being a national – one can't have a positive polarity without a negative – the bad nationalists are still around, but they're in the uncivilised east, something that EU membership has been quite unable to transform, hence the regular assaults on the Central European member states. The Sargentini story is just one among many.

The fear of the national, and it seems to be that, a fear that the universalism of the liberals is under a mounting threat, has begun to generate fascinating counters, namely the slow, quiet, almost clandestine rehabil-itation of empires. Trump and Brexit have been obvious triggers. Any-thing is better than a nation, it would seem.

A clear-cut distinction must be made here between overseas empires (bad) and landward empires, like the Russian, the Ottoman and the Aus-trian empires; these were "good" empires, because they kept nations and nationalism down. I haven't yet seen any attempt to rehabilitate the Ger-man empire, presumably because it is too closely associated with Nazism.

The first time I came across a positive use of empire was in the report issued by the Polish Batory Foundation, the high citadel of liberalism in Warsaw, with the title, "A normative empire in crisis" (2017). I must con-fess that I blinked several times when I saw this, not least because the norms favoured by the report are those of democracy – to me empire and democracy are incompatible – but because I would hardly have expect-ed a good word for empire from a Polish source. Still, we live and learn.

But there is more to come. Krishan Kumar published his *Visions of Empire: How Five Imperial Regimes Shaped the World* in 2017 and he really does seem to think that the Austrian empire was benign, and on-ly benign. Sure enough, he quotes the *Clementia Austriaca*, "the native Austrian mildness and clemency". Predictably, there is no reference to Haynau, to the hanging of the 13 Hungarian generals in Arad and Kos-suth has one mention, in exile as a propagandist. Indeed, the Hungarian element of the empire is all but invisible in this account.

The Russian empire is approvingly described as a multicultural state where liberal reforms after the 1905 revolution (barely mentioned) were putting the country on the right track. Not a word about the post-1905 imperial pacification – over two thousand executions in the Baltic lands alone and at least as many floggings. Very liberal, indeed.

Pieter Judson (*The Hapsburg Empire,* 2016) deals only with the Haps-burgs and, like Kumar, anything that does not support his positive ac-count is omitted. For Kumar, Bach is primarily the composer; Alexander Bach (of the Bach era) is listed as an imperial official. Judson takes it fur-ther, yes, Bach's methods were on the crude side, but after all, he was only promoting the Austrian *mission civilisatrice* during the absolutism of the 1850s in Hungary. A British imperial official praising the administration of India couldn't have put it better. A review of Judson in the *London Review of Books* (30 August 2018) proudly liberates the cat from bag. Judson is right, it asserts, because the Hapsburg empire kept nations, nationhood and nationalism down and it was the right thing to have done. Just imagine someone saying something similar about the colonial wars, like the one France fought in Algeria.

All this suggests that Sargentini is the tip of the iceberg. The liberal current has established its triad of evils and has projected these eastwards. Poland, Hungary et al. are sites of the mounting challenge to liberalism (as currently argued) and are an encouragement to anti-liberals in the West.

And all this raises a further question. Is the EU susceptible to the temptation of empire? It's not difficult to read the Sargentini report as having imperialist overtones, determined to eliminate any view of democracy that contains a national component. Are democracy and nationhood really incompatible? Are Europe and nationhood now to be defined as a mutually exclusive? And, a hard question, does a former empire ever get over its imperial past, its civilising mission, even if the murderous methods of Belgium in the Congo are no longer acceptable? Can the West ever come to terms with those parts of Europe that were subordinated to imperial rule and, hence, have no post-colonial guilt?

But what if?

What if there is more to the picture than what has been sketched so far? Above all, what if the liberal wave – no more than two-three decades old – has peaked? What if the Third Way of the 1990s is coming to its end (nothing lasts for ever) and Europe is entering a new era in which left-liberalism will be just one way of doing politics among many?

What if the accession process has not really delivered on its promises, that of unifying Europe, bringing the West and the East together on fully equal terms? If so, then the resurgence of trust in one's national identity is more readily understood. Indeed, these were the terms on which accession took place, that the EU had competence only where conferral of power had taken place. There is nothing in the treaties banning nationhood.

For the moment, the left-liberal approach is enjoying its hegemony (yes, Gramsci's word), but there is mounting evidence that for growing swathes of opinion the liberal hegemony is no longer exemplary, let alone binding. If we look at the evidence, the real stuff, we get a different picture, at the heart of which the triumph of liberalism is contested – contested with increasing force.

All those dismissed as "populists" are saying no, we want something different, above all, we want a political order in which our voice is heard on equal terms with that of the hegemony which calmly accepts the mounting inequalities that contaminate democracy in Europe.

Nationhood has something to say about this, because it insists on the members of the nation having a certain parity of status. Modern nations emerged in the late 18th century on the argument that all the inhabitants of a given territory were members of the nation with equal rights of political participation.

Besides, this "populism" business is quite odd, if you think about it. Here are people who are regarded as perfectly respectable citizens, upright members of society as members of the demos, but then, when they exercise their democratic right to vote as they choose, they are dissed as "populists" or – to quote the immortal saying by Hillary – they are "deplorables". All it needs is the flick of a switch and out you go, off to the dark side.

It's always difficult to see tectonic change that one is in the midst of, but the shifting plates of the European order ever harder to deny. But this is where Fidesz comes in. The liberal hegemony was always weaker in Central Europe, supported by maybe 10 percent of the voters (on a good day), so that's where the challenge to the hegemony emerged and the alternative was formulated, not least by Fidesz.

As Milan Kundera once wrote, one of the functions of Central Europe is to serve as an early warning system for Europe as a whole. In insisting that liberal free markets generate inequality, Fidesz issued a warning that the free movement of capital and people had negative consequences for states on the semi-periphery. Equally, by blocking the migratory pressure on Europe in 2015, Fidesz demonstrated that a small country could exercise agency even in the face of Europe-wide disapproval. This is what Fidesz has got right and that's why it's so widely detested. Nobody likes a successful prophet, after all.

Hungary after the First World War[*]

History, as is so often repeated, is generally written by the victors. Sometimes, though, the victors are defeated and the suppressed voices of those the victors had intended to cast on the scrapheap of history are heard again. This does not mean the rewriting of the past, an exercise in falsification, but accepting the diversity of how the past is understood and how different eras see their pasts differently.

Secondly, memoir literature must be understood on its own terms. Crucially, it is written within the moral assumptions of its own time, not ours. To repeat L.P. Hartley's oft quoted sentence, "the past is a foreign country: they do things differently there". What the author of a memoir regarded as self-evident modes of feeling and perception are not ours and, given the inevitable psychological remoteness involved, we have to make an effort of interpretation that can go counter to our own assumptions, to our own baggage. If we fail to read the view of the past as seen by contemporaries on their terms, we readily fall into the trap of projecting our moral values onto that past and thereby misjudge it. The temptation to do so is very strong, especially if there is a political or cultural agenda lurking in our assessments.

The communist rulers of Hungary did this consciously and deliberately, for they were seeking actively to rewrite the past for their own needs. The residues of these rewritings have not disappeared. There are

---

* The first part of this text is the introduction to the English translation of Vilmos Nagybaczoni Nagy's memoirs, *Fateful Years* (Helena History Press, 2018). The Afterthoughts are the written version of my contribution made at the book launch on the 18 January 2019.

far too many who paint the past in the darkest hues possible in order to secure their own values in the present. The Hungarian past, not least the interwar period, is widely seen in overwhelmingly negative terms and the actors of that time are written off as fools or knaves, the latter mostly.

This is the significance of the memoirs of Vilmos Nagybaczoni Nagy. It casts a light different from the one insisted on by the communist historians of Hungary on Hungary's role in the Second World War. And because the memoirs were written immediately after the events – first published in 1947 and then republished in 1986 – they have an authenticity and immediacy that the best of memoir literature provides.

What is clear from this account is that Nagybaczoni was well aware of the dilemmas besetting Hungary before and during the War. This demands an analysis and will establish a context in which to place the memoir. Basically the dilemma is that of the small state at risk from the machinations of more powerful international actors and the limits to agency. In the case of Hungary, the dilemma was made more acute by "the loss of empire" syndrome, the Treaty of Trianon, by which pre-1914 Hungary lost two-thirds of its territory and around a third of its indubitably Hungarian population, to which can be added the c.6-7 million non-Hungarians. This was an acute trauma, a defeat for the pre-1914 ruling elite, and a perpetual reminder of the radical reduction in the country's room for manoeuvre.

Furthermore, the end of the First World War was followed by around a year of political chaos (1918–1919) during which incompetent left-wing governments sought to find a way out of the mess and ended up creating an ever larger one. The 133-day Hungarian Soviet Republic was finally put down by the military intervention of the Romanian armed forces, intervention being justified as the defeat of communism and, equally, by the spirit of revanche for the defeat of Romania during the War itself. The occupation of the country by the Romanian army (from August 1919 to March 1920) and the depredations that accompanied it only added to the sense of trauma and humiliation.

Then, before 1914 Hungary was broadly confident of its modernity – still visible in Budapest's architecture – and its particular sense of the future. That future was wholly destroyed by the War and its consequences. During the War, Hungarian casualties were around 800,000 and after Trianon, a substantial number of Hungarians (over 300,000 according to estimates) opted to go to Hungary rather than live in one or other of the successor states; some were expelled. The integration of these returnees, not least members of the state administration dismissed by the successor states, took a long time and added to the trauma. In all, the chaos added up to a collapse – political, economic, social, cultural.

Not surprisingly in the circumstances, the year of chaos effectively destroyed the chances of a social transformation, such as was introduced in neighbouring Austria, and ensured that the pre-1914 elite would return power as the only elite with the necessary political skills and experience. This meant that the pre-1914 social order changed only marginally and remained hierarchical.

Much has been written – mostly negatively – about the backward-looking, "reactionary" character of this elite. This view (favoured by the left) seriously distorts the situation and misstates the problem of consolidation after the year of chaos and the trauma of Trianon. Hungary's political system after Trianon placed stability and security at its centre. The confidence of the pre-1914 period was gone, but it was the only elite with the political skills to reestablish a viable system. This system preserved some of the elements of the pre-1914 order under the aegis of Admiral Horthy as regent. The monarchy remained in being, but there was no agreement as to who the monarch should be; gradually the issue slipped off the agenda. In practice, the system was put together above all by István Bethlen, the prime minister from 1921 to 1931; it was semi-consensual and semi-authoritarian. And there was striking contrast between the modernity of Budapest and the pre- or semi-modernity of the countryside.

The Horthy order allowed a good deal of latitude to the expression of various opinions, as long as the system itself was not threatened. Elections were indeed held to ensure the hegemony of the ruling party and these were neither fully free or fair, but there was competition and parliamentary debates were real enough. By the criteria of the 1920s, the system worked adequately to secure the power of the elite and, equally, to offer some space for alternatives. But it had an Achilles heel, the peasantry, which the country's economy could not really integrate fully. The problem of rural poverty, of the landless peasantry, smallholders and dwarfholders could not be resolved without industrialisation and the country lacked the capital resources to achieve this. Besides, with consolidation as the primary aim, the elites preferred a rather static model of rule – unsurprisingly in the circumstances. It should be added that the competence of the technical intelligentsia and the professional classes was good.

Under the terms of Trianon, Hungary was permitted only a very small army of 35,000, no armour, no heavy weaponry, no air force. This added to the sense of insecurity, given that the system of client states constructed by France – the little Entente – had their own anti-Hungarian perspectives, their own rather more sizeable armies. To this can be added the presence of sizeable Hungarian minorities in the successor states whose attitude to their new citizenship was mixed and whose loyalty was generally questioned by the new rulers. In effect, the country was all but surrounded by ill-disposed, hostile neighbours, which meant that it would need a patron from beyond the region. All the successor states had gained territory from Hungary and had thereby acquired ethnic Hungarian minorities. This created a security problem for the successor states and meant that they necessarily saw Hungary itself as hostile, bent on reacquiring what it had lost. The Western powers, France above all, which had created this vicious circle, never cared about the security issues that would ensue. Everyone was the loser.

This dilemma was well understood by much of the post-1918 elite. It was a severe constraint on action, but it left some room for manoeuvre. Over time, Italy came to play the role of patron with the 1927 accord with Rome. After the 1929 economic crisis and the rise of Hitler, Germany took over. This posed a problem for the elite. Most of them had little time for the radical solutions adopted by Nazism, but there was also a strong pro-German faction. This tension endured and was one of the markers of inter-war Hungarian politics. Clearly, small states had a much more restricted freedom of action and had to align themselves with one or other more powerful state and that affected domestic politics too. The difficulty for the Hungarian elite was that none of the potential patrons was particularly interested in the central Hungarian issue – the injustice of Trianon and the insecurity that came with it. If anything, France and to a lesser extent Britain were content to see Hungary on a leash; any attachment to the Soviet Union was obviously out of question given the country's experience with the communist experiment in 1919; Weimar Germany was not interested, which left Italy as the only player, albeit the newly launched Fascist system under Mussolini was unattractive to the conservatism of the dominant elites.

The 1930s economic crisis hit the country very hard. The massive shrinkage of the international market left the economy in a poor state. In any case, Hungary was far too heavily dependent on agriculture – up to two-fifths of the GDP and over half the population – and remained capital poor. The structure of the agricultural sector was dominated by underfunded large estates, the latifundia, and it lost much of its export markets with the crash. There was some small sector production, but this too suffered from capital shortage and technological backwardness. The outcome was an insoluble peasant problem. The country was described, with only some exaggeration, as the land of "three million beggars".

By 1932 the conservative elite associated with Horthy and Bethlen effectively found itself incapable of dealing with the crisis of growing social discontent, the short-lived government of Gyula Károlyi resigned and in 1932, Gyula Gömbös, a contested figure if ever there was one, took over as prime minister. Gömbös was a right-radical figure with a military background, but he recognised that the strategy of stability followed in the post-Trianon years was exhausted. Broadly, he sought to revitalise the country by launching his National Work Programme which aimed at the modernisation and rationalisation of the public sphere. This included social reforms and attention to the peasantry. He was also successful in rejuvenating the army with the retirement of 22 senior officers in 1935. In foreign policy, Gömbös launched various openings, the net effect of which was to move the country closer to Germany; he was not alone at the time in admiring the dynamism of Nazism, whether in Hungary or elsewhere. All the same, the alignment was not total and there remained some choices. Not least, the conservative elite around Bethlen, together with the Smallholders and Social Democrats, were less than delighted with this course and opposed it.

Gömbös died in 1936, but his mobilising, reform policies were not altogether successful. Above all, both he and the conservatives were increasingly challenged by various right radical movements. The opening of the franchise made the Hungarian variant of Nazism, the Arrow Cross, a serious problem for the adherents of stability and equally for the moderate right. In any case, as Gömbös's successors were to discover, Germany's growing political and economic dominance meant a growing constraint on what the country could do.

For the elites, whether conservative or right-radical and to some extent even the relatively weak Social Democrats, the question of Trianon and frontier revision was central. There was agreement on this revision being peaceful, but there was division on whether Hungary should aim for total revision – everything back – or only the indubitably Hungarian inhabited areas. Revision necessarily brought the country closer to Germany and Italy, given that neither was satisfied with the Paris Peace Settlement.

The year 1938 was a turning point. With Anschluß, Germany had become a direct neighbour and the Munich agreement created an opportunity to satisfy the revisionist claim against the disintegrating Czechoslovakia by reattaching the overwhelmingly Hungarian-inhabited strip of southern Slovakia. Germany and Italy were the midwives of this agreement, the first Vienna Arbitration, but Hitler regarded Hungary as a troublesome, not altogether reliable semi-satellite. Much the same applied to the second Vienna Arbitration, when around of two-fifths of Transylvania was returned to Hungary from Romania. In the interim, Hungary reoccupied Sub-Carpathian Ruthenia and, following Germany's attack on Yugoslavia in 1941, the Bácska (Bačka) region of the Vojvodina.

Hungary was able to remain neutral during this period, though closely attached to the Axis, but that ended when the town and airport of Kassa (Košice) were bombed (26 June 1941). Horthy decided that the Soviet Union was responsible and entered the war. (Who was actually responsible remains a mystery. The least implausible theory is that Soviet planes bombed Kassa in error, intending to attack the nearby Eperjes (Prešov) in Slovakia instead.) Hungary's participation in the war lasted until 1945, but with the destruction of the Second Hungarian Army at Voronezh in January 1943, it was hardly an active role. The story ended with the Red Army invading Hungary in 1944, the siege of Budapest, far-reaching devastation and a collapse as deep-seated as that after 1918. It is against this background that Nagybaczoni's career and memoirs are to be understood.

Nagybaczoni was born in 1884 in Transylvania, his family was of rather poor lesser nobility and Calvinist. He received his education at the Ludovika and Vienna military academies, fought on the Serbian and Russian fronts in the First World War and remained in military service after Trianon, reaching the rank of colonel in 1925. He wrote regularly on military strategy and tactics and was promoted to major-general (vezérőrnagy) in 1934, to lieutenant-general (altábornagy) in 1937, was commander of the Budapest army corps in 1938.

It was in this function that he took part in the military occupation of southern Slovakia and, as commander-in-chief of the First Hungarian Army, of northern Transylvania. This was evidently a distinguished career, but Nagybaczoni had his opponents, chief among Henrik Werth, chief of staff, who succeeded in having Nagybaczoni sent into retirement in 1941. Werth was strongly pro-German, was of the view that Germany could not lose the war and objected to those, Nagybaczoni among them, who harboured doubts on this score.

Indeed, as he makes evident in the memoir, Nagybaczoni was of the view that war would be a disaster for Hungary. There was a clear rivalry between the two senior soldiers. Werth, however, lost the contest and with the coming to office of the Kállay government in 1942, Nagybaczoni was appointed minister of defence. Kállay recognised that the German war was doomed and he pursued a semi-neutral policy, in the hope that after the war, this would gain recognition and Hungary would not be as badly treated as after 1918. This was illusory, of course, given the determination of the Allies to wage a war of unconditional surrender. And Kállay's policies brought Hungary increasingly into Hitler's bad books, which culminated in the German occupation of the country in March 1944.

As defence minister (1942–1943) Nagybaczoni was responsible for various moves to improve the condition of the Hungarian armed forces, above all, his determination to end the inhuman treatment of Jews. One of the anti-Jewish measures introduced in 1939–1941 was that Jews could not serve in the regular armed forces but were required to do labour service (munkaszolgálat). This service was coercive, those serving were unarmed, and the guards regularly treated Jews with marked inhumanity. It should be added that those obliged to do coercive labour service included non-Jews, so-called unreliable elements, communists, Roma, members of ethnic minorities, but the majority, several hundred thousand, were Jewish.

Nagybaczoni tried, and to some extent succeeded, in diminishing this brutality, but the degree of anti-Semitism in military and civilian circles was deeply rooted. His measures generated growing opposition among the right-radicals of the pro-German elements and they succeeded in forcing into Nagy retirement in 1943. On the 15 October 1944, with the collapse of the Horthy system, the Arrow Cross seized power and a day later, they arrested Nagybaczoni, imprisoned him, moved him to Germany as the front was disintegrating in 1945 and he was only able to return to Hungary well after the end of the war. It was then that he wrote this memoir.

His tribulations were not over. The communist regime regarded him as a class enemy, stripped him of his pension and his work as a gardener. But chance intervened. Petru Groza, the then Romanian head of state, had been a class mate of Nagybaczoni's at the Szászváros (Orăştie) Secondary School, they graduated together, and Groza invited him to the 50th anniversary of the graduating class. Nagybaczoni replied that he had neither the money nor the passport and Groza then intervened with Rákosi, the communist leader, who allowed Nagybaczoni to take part and the authorities gradually lifted the restrictions that they had imposed on him. In 1965, his actions to improve the treatment of Jewish forced labourers during the war were recognised by Israel and he was awarded the title of "righteous among nations". Nagybaczoni died in 1976 at the age of 92.

Two thoughts can be added to these memoirs. One of these is that Nagybaczoni's life was characterised by professionalism and a fundamental decency. As a serving soldier, he accepted that his duties were military and not political, whether he accepted the views of the political leadership or not, but only up to a given point. While he recognised that Hungary's situation left it and him with few choices, within those constraints he acted as thoughtfully as was possible to mitigate human suffering and to minimise damage.

The second thought that comes to mind is that while the interwar elites of Hungary were far from flawless, they were not the consummate villains depicted by the communist period. Some certainly were, notably the hardline, pro-German anti-Semites, but the majority of the elite sought to sustain a degree of moderation and propriety. That elite was swept away by the Second World War and their successors did what they could to blacken their predecessors. But history is not carved in stone and today we can or, at any rate have the capacity to, adopt a different, more nuanced understanding of the past. After all, the current elites will also be judged by their successors. So when making judgements of the past, it is always worth doing so with care and moderation. I am certain that Nagybaczoni would have endorsed this and would have done so firmly and rigorously. That was his character.

Afterthoughts: the long shadow of Trianon

The question that arises from all this concerns the nature and quality of the Hungarian state that Nagybaczoni found himself in. He was self-evidently committed to Hungary and, despite his Transylvanian birth, he would not have been at all welcome in the new Romanian state, indeed, he might well have been treated as a war criminal.

The Hungarian state that came into being with the end of the first world war can justly be described as traumatised by a series of cumulative caesuras that made coming to terms with itself a near-impossible task. The country declared its full independence on the 17 October 1918, though maintaining the Hapsburg monarch in a personal union. The republic was proclaimed on the 16 November (monarchy was restored on 1 March 1920). It is noteworthy that none of these dates has any resonance in the Hungarian memory regime, and whereas most of the states of Central Europe celebrated their centenary of independence in 2018, Hungary did not. The implication is that this independence is or was charged with ambivalence and was attained at an intolerably high price.

First, there were the war losses, the humiliation of having lost the war and the approximately one million dead, wounded and missing during the fighting. Demobilised soldiers returned in no particular order and found the country beset by severe shortages. Prisoners of war began to trickle back gradually, for some, from Russia, this could take years. The state was badly placed to make any provision for them. To these human losses can be added the roughly 150,00 who died from the Spanish flu pandemic.

Then, the war effort placed serious strains on both the economy and the state administration. Hungary was in any case the most backward part of Austria-Hungary and had faced a shortage of capital and entrepreneurial skills even before 1914. The wholly unequal distribution of land – the latifundia run sub-optimally – meant that the returning soldiers, mostly of peasant stock, had every cause for complaint. This basically meant that Hungary would remain beset by capital shortage and that squeezing consumption to finance industrialisation (as Taiwan and South Korea did well after the second world war) was not an option. The result was rural poverty, inequality, few avenues of upward mobility, discontent and a peasant population that was vulnerable to radical mobilisation, not really caring whether this came from the left or the right.

As Pál Hatos has described in his excellent "The Accursed Republic" (*Az elátkozott köztárs*aság), the immediate return of several hundred thousand demobbed soldiers was a collapse of order and a peasant uprising. The elite that had led Hungary during the war threw in the towel and accepted that a new republican system would be launched. This new elite resembled the old, in as much as it drew heavily on the aristocracy, Mihály Károlyi himself obviously, as well as the radical left.

The new republican order failed miserably, a failure that was accentuated by the elite's utter inability to recognise that with the defeat, historic Hungary was finished and that the non-Magyar population would secede. Their second failure was to misperceive the war aims of the Entente and to believe that Woodrow Wilson's 14 points applied to them and to Hungarians. There was a kind of obstinate credulousness in the elite, in insisting that the Entente would treat defeated Hungary even-handedly and not favour the newly fledged members of the entente – Czechoslovakia, the South Slav kingdom and Romania.

They were proved disastrously mistaken in believing that the Entente would even listen to their arguments about the c. 3 million Magyars who were being transferred to the successor states without their consent. The reality that these non-consensual citizens (subjects?) would prove to be an irritant in the new, ethnically organised states did not trouble either the successor states or their Western patrons. These new minorities could, it was thought, be integrated, assimilated or suppressed. It took a long time to recognise that an ethnically conscious population that had undergone some experience of modernity (in their mother tongue) would remain attached to that culture and not exchange it in any large numbers.

If the October-November 1918 republic was a dismal failure, what followed, the 133-day Hungarian Soviet Republic, turned out to be even worse. The new leaders sought to impose their radical solutions immediately and intransigently, they regarded questioning or criticism as treason (they were persuaded that history was on their side, after all, Lenin had said as much). Béla Kun's attempt to re-establish a communist Greater Hungary had some initial military success, but alarmed the Entente, which then gave the green light to the successor states to intervene, meaning to invade Hungary. The Romanian army broke the Hungarian Red Army with comparative ease, captured Budapest on the 3-4 August 1919 and proceeded to occupy almost the entire territory of Hungary, leaving Budapest in November and eastern Hungary, the lands east of the Tisza, only in March 1920 – one of Romania's war aims was the Tisza as the country's western frontier, a topos that still resurfaces in the 21st century. This was too much even for the Entente and the Romanian army was ordered to evacuate Hungary. This it did, leaving behind considerable chaos, and a memory of numerous summary executions and depredations.

The end of the occupation meant that the question of what kind of political system Hungary should have returned to the agenda. There was a brief attempt to set up a Social Democrat government, but the Romanians quickly put a stop to that and eventually handed over power to the conservative elite led by Admiral Horthy, presumably at the behest of the Entente, which did take over and gradually re-established a degree of order. During the 1919 Soviet period, the Red Terror claimed numerous victims; now a White Terror claimed even more. To be precise, the White Terror – the summary executions of those thought to have supported the Soviet republic – was begun by the Romanian occupation forces.

But Horthy's government had a further caesura to undergo – to sign the peace treaty with the Entente. Most of the terms were already agreed by the latter in 1919, hence there were no substantive negotiations before the signing of the Treaty of Trianon. This meant the loss of around two-thirds of the territory of historic Hungary and some 13 million people, of whom – as noted – around 3 million were indisputably ethnic Hungarians. The dual loss of territory and population was a profound shock which overshadowed Hungarian politics until 1945.

The recovery of some of the territory and people between 1938 and 1940 was followed by their renewed loss after 1945. The trauma of Trianon would certainly have been eased had the ethnically Magyar population been given the choice of staying with Hungary or with the successor states, but this was never an option whether in 1920 or 1945–1947 (the date of the Paris Peace treaty that ended world war two belligerency). And with the defeat and destruction of 1944–1945, the historic elite was utterly discredited. Its policy of reversing Trianon disappeared with it, so territorial revisionism has had no purchase in Hungarian national consciousness since.

Horthy basically reinstituted a shrunken version of the system that had existed before 1914, it was a pluralist system run by a hegemonic party – the government party – with a public administration that functioned tolerably in the urban areas, but left the countryside more or less untouched. There was a schooling system, most of the population was literate, but much of the rural population was at or just above subsistence level, with few chances of escape.

Given the composition of the elite, the pre-1914 aristocracy, land reform was inconceivable and, it should be added, would not have solved the peasant problem, as the rural population exceeded the amount of land that could be distributed and farmed efficiently. Nor could industry be developed to absorb the surplus rural population, given the unavailability of investment capital and skills. What this meant was that a sizeable section of the c.3 million peasantry was pre-political and lacked the forms of knowledge needed for modernity, let alone the civic skills required for democracy.

But what it did have, and this was true of the entire population, was a strong sense of the national self, of Hungarian nationhood and to a degree of Trianon itself. Indeed, it is hard to see how the country could have held together without this sense of national consciousness, even if this national self had a weak belief in agency at the individual level, an acceptance of hierarchy (together with resistance to hierarchy) and pessimism about collective agency. After all, Hungary had been denied all agency at Trianon and the somewhat flawed concept of Hungarian modernity, including a sense of civilising mission in the Danube valley (borrowed from France), had disintegrated.

Then, the Hungary that emerged after Trianon was a non-consensual state, in as much as the massive loss of territory was traumatising and not accepted by the elites and much of political society. There was, however, agreement that the regaining of territory would have to be secured legally, which brought up the question of how this might happen. It was well understood in Budapest that no state would voluntarily hand over territory which it regarded as its own. This necessarily meant pressure from a stronger outside power, given that the League of Nations was incapable of doing anything of the kind. It goes without saying, that Hungary's neighbours were well aware of all this, meaning that throughout the interwar period, there was a severe security problem in Central Europe. And none of the parties had an interest in resolving it.

Finally, the nature of the hegemonic international system was heavily weighted against the losers of the World War. Not only were they treated as losers, but they were expected to construct and sustain democratic systems in circumstances when both the international and the domestic factors were pointing in the opposite direction. The newly established League of Nations (1920) was supposed to resolve the inevitable conflicts that arise when a sizeable number of states operates in a geographically constricted area (Europe), but in practice it was dominated by the interests of the great powers of the winning side.

Thus France ran its own system of client states in Central Europe, the Little Entente, the explicit purpose of which was to ensure that Hungary, Austria and Germany would remain in a subordinate position and thereby guarantee the security of France's clients only. The proposition that security might be mutual existed only at the verbal level. In this context, while Germany – given its size – could never be fully isolated, Hungary could and was, leaving Budapest with very few options for building its own security.

The opening towards Italy, which saw itself as having emerged from the war without adequate compensation, was a partial answer, as Italy proved ready to play a role as patron. But this hardly meant the integration of Hungary into a European system on equal terms, indeed, it continued to be seen as a destabilising factor, given its revisionism, its territorial claims on all its neighbours. As far as international systems were concerned, it's worth adding that Germany took over Italy's role in the 1930s, with dire consequences, then Hungary was forcibly integrated into the Soviet system and thereafter into the Western system. NATO and EU accession gave Hungary a new system to the rules of which it could accede, but over time, found itself at odds with Brussels on a number of issues, above all on the question of the distribution of power between the EU and its member states.

Historical causation is always difficult to establish, hence it would be going too far to draw a direct line from the cumulative traumas of 1918-1920 to the present, even adding those of 1944-1945 (first German, then Soviet occupation, the far-reaching physical destruction), the imposition of communist power and the coercive transformation of social, economic and political structures, and the revolution of 1956 that ended in failure.

The pre-1945 concept of the Hungarian state was heavily invested in the recovery of lost territory and structured state independence around this objective. The shattering defeat of 1944–1945 buried this concept and showed how contingent that independent statehood was and, indeed, could be lost. As in fact it was with the gradual arrival of Soviet control, in place by 1948. Hence in 1956, during the revolution, not only was neutrality of the state one of the declared aims of the Imre Nagy government, but at the popular level, the slogan of "Russians go home" (*Ruszkik haza*) had widespread resonance. Point 14 of the demands of the revolutionaries included the use of the national coat of arms (instead of the hammer and wheatsheaf introduced by the communists), a military uniform in accordance with the national traditions and that the 15 March, the anniversary of the 1848 revolution, be declared a holiday.

The clear inference is that Hungarian statehood was now seen as a value with which society identified, the transfrontier communities had lost their significance and Hungarian society had come to terms with itself within the Trianon frontiers. After 1989, the dilemma of independent sovereign statehood and how to structure it became a matter of the international system into which Hungary was to be integrated. There was never any doubt that this would be NATO and the EU.

Nevertheless, one can see a certain continuity in the Hungarian story, which helps to explain the sensitivity of one tradition, that of the national conservative right, which is suspicious of external interference in the national state's agency, and equally, the rejection of this by the left which believes that Hungary's only viable future is the acceptance of subalternity, of the demands of the hegemonic international system, given that attempts at autonomous agency have resulted in failure. The outcome of these irreconcilable definitions of the Hungarian national self is a polarisation that, at this time, cannot be bridged. But what is unquestionable is that a Hungarian national identity exists, it is sustained by its own myth-symbol complex and memory regimes and will not disappear. This identity is closely linked to Hungary's statehood and in that sense has changed from the attitudes of 1918–1920. There is an acceptance of the Trianon frontiers and, equally, that the transfrontier Hungarians are somehow linked to Hungary, but have different cultural trajectories, even when the latter have Hungarian citizenship.

A part of the problem is that language confuses as much as it clarifies. Statehood, nationhood are thoroughly mingled in the Hungarian case, this confusion being the legacy of Trianon. In that respect, a certain ambivalence about the limits of statehood and nationhood remains in being. The transfer of three million ethnic Hungarians who were aware of their relationship to the Hungarian state has sustained this ambiguity and ambivalence. In what way is the Hungarian identity of a transfrontier Hungarian to be assessed and by whom? These questions remain open. The connection between Hungarian society in Hungary and the transfrontier Hungarians was officially buried during the communist period, but it never disappeared from popular consciousness, not least by reason of the ambiguity.

The link was transmitted by family, individual and other memory systems, like literature and the myth-symbol complex. Thus the post-1945 expulsion of c. 95,000 ethnic Hungarians from Slovakia was a part of the secret knowledge of those affected, though never acknowledged publicly. It was a form of knowledge that went against the grain of communist internationalism. Overall, the population of Hungary was never fully disconnected from their transfrontier co-ethnics. After 1989, this issue became a major divide between right and left; indeed, one of the founding narratives of the Hungarian right is that it cares for all Hungarians, regardless of the state in which they live (Antall proclaimed himself the prime minister of 15 million Hungarians). The left defined itself against this, and in the referendum of 2004, it campaigned against the transfrontier Hungarians having anything to do with Hungary. It is in this sense that state independence is still marked by ambivalence, because the relationship between statehood and nationhood is unresolved and, for that matter, cannot be resolved given the structural factors. This is the long shadow of Trianon.

2019

EU Law and Politics: the Rule of Law Framework[*]

The Commission's new rule of law mechanism, called a "Framework", was communicated to the EU Council on the 11 March 2014 and attracted next to no attention until now. The date is not entirely insignificant – it was issued just before the 2014 elections to the European Parliament and largely escaped notice. At first sight, what is equally difficult to explain is why the Framework never emerged in the context of Hungary, long a bête noire of the Western left and the object of several infringement procedures launched by the Commission.

In December 2015, when the legal affairs commissioner, Věra Jourová, concluded the plenary debate on Hungary, she mentioned the Framework, but stated, "The Commission has at this stage not activated the Rule of Law Framework as regards Hungary." And then added, "Considering that concerns about the situation in Hungary are being addressed by a range of infringement procedures and pre-infringement procedures, and that also the Hungarian justice system has a role to play, the Commission takes the view that the conditions to activate the Rule of Law Framework regarding Hungary are at this stage not met."

So, somewhat to the irritation of some (left-wing) MEPs, the Commission's view of Hungary was fairly emollient – whenever problems arose, she argued in effect, these were sorted out through dialogue with the Hungarian government. For what it's worth, the Framework was never brought up in Parliament's Constitutional Affairs committee either.

---

[*] Published online at http://verfassungsblog.de/eu-law-and-politics-the-rule-of-law-framework.

The core of the Framework is that action must be taken if, in the Commission's view, there is systemic risk to the rule of law in a member state, stress being on systemic, meaning that one-off breaches are not relevant. The definition of systemic is in the hands of the Commission.

The procedure itself establishes four principles for action – dialogue, an assessment of what is actually happening in the member state, equal treatment of all member states and concrete action to remedy the situation in order to avoid an Article 7 process. Only if it thinks that there does actually exist a systemic risk, "the Commission will assess the possibility of activating one of the mechanisms set out in Article 7".

Much of the media and political comment has sought to establish a kind of twinning between Hungary and Poland, that the latter was simply following the (bad) example of the former – a kind of liberal guilt by association maybe. So the question then arises, why be fairly emollient with Hungary, but to reach for the Framework in the case of Poland?

There are no convincing answers. Legally, there are some differences between the two countries, even if politically they are widely seen as alike. But based on precedent, dialogue and possibly infringement procedures ought to have been enough when dealing with Poland. Instead, the activation of Framework indicates that one legal procedure has been replaced by another, but this time political, action – again it's unclear why.

The proposition that there is a political element involved is underscored by the fact that the Polish government had asked the Venice Commission for legal advice. The Commission chose not to wait for that to arrive.

The situation was made hazier yet by diverging reports on what the College of Commissioners actually decided. According to some reports, there was a decision by the College not to launch the Framework, but to establish the facts of what has happened in Poland first. This was not what was announced at the press conference that followed, on the contrary.

Certainly, the Juncker Commission declared itself to be a political one, so politics appears to have primacy over legal procedures. If so, a political assessment of the decision is more than justified. And that assessment has to begin from the Commission being the guardian of Treaties – even if a political guardian is something new.

All this is odd, just the same. It's common ground that one of the most sensitive areas of activity in the public sphere is where law and politics meet. The Commission has been particularly insistent that its actions are governed by law. Anything else would obviously be arbitrary and destructive. This seems to be especially clear-cut when questions of the rule of law are on the agenda.

So the oddity is that what we have is a rule of law mechanism, the Framework, being employed for political purposes. This bodes ill for the future, because it will generate resistance, erode respect for the rule of law and provide fuel for Eurosceptics, and that would seem to be completely counter-productive from the Commission's standpoint.

This prioritisation of politics over law in the relationship between the Commission and a member state has already arisen once, in November 2015 to be precise, when the Commission gave the go-ahead to a European Citizens' Initiative (ECI) aimed at triggering an Article 7 procedure against Hungary.

Article 7, as everyone knows by now or should, is a long, slow, laborious process at the end of which a sinful member state is deprived of its voting rights. To get there, it has to be determined that there is "a clear risk of a serious breach by a Member State" of the principles laid out in Article 2 of the Treaty. Article 7 lays down three steps. In the first instance, starting from "a reasoned proposal" by one third of the member states or by the Commission or by the European Parliament, there has to be a decision by a four-fifths majority in Council that there is a risk of a serious breach. The second step requires a decision by unanimity and the consent of the European Parliament. After this, Council can act by a qualified majority. So the demand made by an ECI to launch an Article 7 procedure seems unlikely to succeed, given the hurdles.

Now it so happens that I am well versed in the world of the ECI, having been Parliament's rapporteur on the instrument. There is no question that hitherto the Commission has been extremely cautious in accepting ECIs, and cautious is an understatement. Then, ECIs are there to impel the Commission to formulate legislation on some issue of general EU concern. *The Right to Water* (R2W) initiative is a good example.

Yet out of nothing, the Commission accepted the ECI launched by *Wake up Europe*, namely "We call on the EU to go further and trigger the procedure laid out in the Treaty of European Union (Article 7) to check whether the Orbán government policies and legislative changes respect European values."

I cannot in any way see what this has to do with formulating legislation, implying that the Commission accepted the *Wake up Europe* initiative for political reasons, as a move against Hungary. My guess is, by the way, that the initiative will fail in that it is unlikely to mobilise one million signatures by next November (within one year) and if it does, it will be taken to the Luxembourg Court (the ECJ) by the Hungarian government.[1] Law and politics meet again, and it's not a very happy get-together.

There is worse to come, though. There are grave doubts about the Commission's Framework having any legal basis at all. In May 2014, the legal service of Council explicitly and emphatically announced that "there is no legal basis in the Treaties empowering the institutions [of the EU] to create a new supervision mechanism of the respect of the rule of law by the Member States", other than what is prescribed in Article 7. Council's legal service then goes on to suggest that a Member State peer review of the rule of law could be compatible with the Treaties.

To complicate matters further in the area of rule of law breaches, Council did agree to something like the suggested peer review and holds regular "conversations" on the topic. At the same time, the European Parliament has also embarked on establishing a rule of law mechanism, which is likely to be voted on in July this year. How these three separate instruments will be synchronised is unclear and, quite apart from anything, none of them will have a legal basis unless and until there is treaty change.

---

1   The call has indeed been withdrawn since then.

Treaty change, however, has become one of the most difficult of exercises in the EU. The Lisbon Treaty evidently can't be the last such EU treaty, but treaty revision is necessarily is an extended process. It requires the calling of a Convention, and it will be politically impossible to limit the agenda to one or two issues. Once a draft is agreed, it must then be accepted by the European Council and then goes for ratification to all the member states (around 40 chambers, minus two if the UK leaves) and by the European Parliament. Referenda are legally obligatory in the Irish Republic and politically so in several other member states. There is no guarantee that these referenda will approve the putative new treaty if the 2005 precedents are anything to go by, when French and Dutch voters rejected the Constitutional Treaty agreed at the previous Convention. It is no surprise that most Brussels insiders blench at the mention of treaty change.

One could go on speculating as to what is really going on currently. Steps have been taken by the Commission to secure the health of the rule of law in Poland, yet this has been done in a non-legal way – there would seem to be quite a contradiction here. The legal and political factors should clearly be separate, yet appear to be intertwined and that augurs badly, in that it could generate confusion and potentially introduce political criteria in the assessment of breaches of the rule of law.

At the same time, media reporting of the Framework, Poland, Hungary and all has been superficial and partisan, to put it mildly. Is it conceivable that the Commission decided to use the Framework in the case of Poland because of pressure by the media and, maybe, some member states?

Then, from the Central European perspective, many will conclude that the EU is picking on Poland and Hungary and that, in turn, does nothing to strengthen the credibility or the neutrality of the EU. In this context, it would really help if the Commission were to place one of the Western states in the cross-hairs of the Framework – there are skeletons everywhere, after all.

References

Situation in Hungary: follow-up to the European Parliament Resolution of 10 June 2015 (debate), http://www.europarl.europa.eu/sides/getDoc.do?type=CRE&reference=20151202&secondRef=ITEM-017&language=EN

Right2water CAMPAIGN | From the European Citizens Initiative to the Global Water Justice Campaign, https://www.eapn.eu/water-campaign/

Wake up Europe! Humanists Launch a European Citizens' Initiative to Sanction Hungary! https://humanistfederation.eu/wake-europe-humanists-launch-european-citizens-initiative-sanction-hungary/

Commission's Communication on a new EU Framework to strengthen the Rule of Law: compatibility with the Treaties, http://data.consilium.europa.eu/doc/document/ST-10296-2014-INIT/en/pdf

28 Feb 2016

Nationhood, Modernity, Democracy: Manifestations of National Identity in Modern Europe*

The modern nation is the central and most effective guarantor of democracy. For many, this proposition is challenging, provocative, and perhaps even offensive. The world is full of idealists who believe in the superiority of universal norms that all should accept. My position is that this is utopian, possibly the road to dystopia, because all ideas, all ideals, utopias, ways of seeing or improving the world are culturally coded and, therefore, represent a particular and particularist perspective. And to impose one particularist perspective onto another is the high road to despotism. One of my underlying assumptions is that all cultures are communities of moral value – they create moral values and demand recognition as communities of value creation and worth.[1] And if we accept this proposition, then it follows that we place a value on diversity, however much we may dislike certain practices that other communities of moral worth pursue. This position, however, is directly challenged by globalization and human rights normativity, for instance, and the world that we live in can be interpreted along this polarity.

Centrally, there is constant tension between universalistic and particularistic discourses. It would be sad indeed if either were to triumph over the other. Both are needed. Universalism threatens to become oppressive

---

* Paper delivered in Minneapolis, Minnesota, 2001, http://epa.niif.hu/00400/00476/00006/pdf/005-017.pdf.

1 Robert Wuthnow, *Meaning and Moral Order: Explorations in Cultural Analysis* (Berkeley, CA: University of California Press, 1987).

unless challenged by ideas external to it and the same applies to particularism. But since the Enlightenment, we in the West have tended to privilege universalism and universalistic discourses and have tended unconsciously to assume that what we think is what all right-minded people think. Not so. The world is infinitely diverse and various.

Our views of the world, however much they may assume the guise of representing the most enlightened approach, are nevertheless bounded. None of us is culturally innocent. If this is so, then the role of culture and cultural diversity must be accepted as having a positive role in sustaining values that are meaningful. Indeed, if there is one thing that is universal, it is diversity itself.

In the argument that follows, I want to take a very close look at the relationship between political power and cultural community. The pivot of my argument is that this relationship is real, that political power rests on bounded cultures, and that the very real attainments of democracy are determined to a significant extent by the cultural foundations of political power.

My starting point is the arrival of modernity. Modernity is a much contested concept; it has dimensions in politics, economics, society, and culture in the widest sense, not to mention in psychology and other areas. In the context of nationhood, however, the central determinant is the transformation of the nature of power. From the seventeenth century, the early modern state underwent a significant shift in its contours and capacities. It radically increased its power over the inhabitants of the territories it controlled and began a process of territorial consolidation to secure this new-found power.[2] This shift took place for a number of interlocking reasons, mostly to do with the introduction of new technologies of information storage, military potential, and methods of organization. The information revolution of the sixteenth century was based, of course, on the invention of printing in the previous century; it consist-

---

2   John Breuilly, "The State and Nationalism", in Montserrat Guibernau and John Hutchinson (eds.), *Understanding Nationalism* (Cambridge: Polity, 2001), 32–52.

ed in the application of this technology to the recording capacity of the state, creating the possibility of large-scale bureaucracies and the corresponding emergence of increased rate of literacy. The outcome was what we have come to know as the absolutist state.

These practices were paralleled by the rapid growth of the scientific sphere – scientific in the widest sense of knowledge – that was to find full form in the Enlightenment of the eighteenth century. By the mid-eighteenth century, Europe was the home to a growing number of people with the literacy, the knowledge, and the aspirations to constitute what today we would call an intellectual elite.[3] This was the Republic of Letters. Simultaneously, new trading and production patterns, equally reliant on literacy, were resulting in a growing accumulation of wealth in private hands. This posed a problem for the state. Taxing the newly moneyed entrepreneurial classes would appear to offer new opportunities for extending the power of the state, but it was already understood that taxation without a *quid pro quo* was ineffective: people did not like to be taxed without their consent. In England, this issue had already come to the fore during the 1640s and was a key aspect of the civil war. Similarly, the state discovered that people did not care to be coerced without their consent.

The question then arose of how, and to what extent, the state would redistribute power in order to attain the consent of the governed. It is in this moment that we can see the origins of citizenship and democracy. Without consent, there can be no democracy, of course. In the Thirteen Colonies, this proposition generated the slogan: "no taxation without representation". Note that this was an extraordinarily radical idea, one that ran directly counter to the accepted order of access to political power as the exclusive privilege of birth, in other words, the aristocracy.

The first beneficiaries of the new concept of governance found that the combination of these forces – rule by a degree of consent, economic power in the private sphere, intellectual exchange – allowed them access to disproportionate power. This was Britain and the Netherlands, to

---

3   Zygmunt Bauman, *Legislators and Interpreters* (Cambridge: Polity, 1987).

some extent France before the revolution, and Switzerland. But the picture also had its dark side. Rule by consent immediately raised the problem of dissent. What would happen if a significant group of people chose not to consent, to demand access to power of their own? Should they be able to establish a new state? In pre-modernity, when state power was looser, this was not a serious issue. States could arise and disappear – this was the fate of Burgundy, for example. But once power, people, and territory came together as the central resource, no holder of power would willingly countenance its disruption.

To cement these newly modernizing states, therefore, something else was needed. Ideal-typically, to answer the problem of dissent, a shared culture had to be constructed which was sufficiently cohesive to pre-empt dissent and disruption. With modernity, no state would willingly countenance the loss of power and prestige that secession represented. The early modern state attained this by a combination of ethnic cleansing, oppression and assimilation of culturally deviant groups. France eliminated the Protestant Huguenots with the revocation of the Edict of Nantes. England marginalized English and Irish Catholics; in the Netherlands, again, Catholics were held down. And the United States began its international career by eliminating about a third of its population, the Loyalists who remained committed to the British Crown. This also points towards something else – the growing role of secularization by the eighteenth century.

The modern state, in order to attain the degree of cultural homogeneity that would permit political heterogeneity, had to condense sufficient cultural power to make this act of coercion relatively risk-free. Sections of the population regarded as posing a potential risk had to be made to conform to a state-driven and elite-driven model of cultural and moral normativity. The state, therefore, took over some of the normative goal-setting that religion had performed until then and assumed the role primary agent of cohesion.[4] In exchange, citizenship of-

---

4   On the significance of coherence creation, see Mircea Eliade, *The Myth of the Eternal Return: Cosmos and History* (London: Penguin, 1954), and Csaba Pléh, "A narrativumok mint a pszichológiai koherenciateremtés eszközei" [Narratives as instruments for creating psychological coherence], *Holmi* 8/2, Feb. 1996, 265–282.

fered access to political power and the wider world of literacy, education, and choice.

The question arises whether this newly devised state-driven set of
norms could be purely or overwhelmingly civic, requiring no solidarity of the type that we would define today as ethnic? Initially, the situation was unclear and the early narratives were certainly civic. The French
revolution invented the *citoyen*, making all inhabitants of the territory
of France potential members of the French nation; however, there was
always a preference for the language of the Ile de France. Could one be
a citizen of France while speaking Breton? No. Similarly in Britain, the
idea that one could speak Welsh in the public sphere and assume full
rights using that language would have been dismissed as laughable until
the 1960s. From the outset, therefore, non-civic elements were brought
into nationhood and citizenship was conjoined with language, thereby
necessarily importing the non-philological qualities of language into citizenship.[5] It is dangerously naive to suppose that a language can be neutral in this respect. However, this did not and does not mean that a state
must be monolingual, just that life is much easier if this is the case.

From this perspective, the idea of the civic contract as the determinant of the nature of the modern state was always a myth, a self-serving narrative. Citizenship is a cold concept. Legal regulation, administrative procedures, rights and entitlements do not build solidarity and
trust. Citizenship needs a cultural foundation and cultures have qualities of their own that cut across the ostensible goals of full and equal citizenship for all the residents of a state territory.[6]

The problem with basing civic rights exclusively on residence, taxation and obeying the law, as universalists like to do, is that it ignores the
tacit norms, the implicit bases of consent. As children of the Enlightenment, we like to believe that we are in possession of a seamless universal

5   Yuri M. Lotman, *Universe of the Mind: A Semiotic Theory of Culture*, trans. Anne Shukman (London:
     I.B. Tauris, 2001).
6   Christopher G.A. Bryant, "Civic Nation, Civil Society, Civil Religion", in John Hall (ed.), *Civil Soci-
     ety: Theory, History, Comparison* (Cambridge: Polity, 1995), 136–157.

rationality. This is a fallacy. It assumes either that cultures are so alike that all differences can be ironed out without any damage or difficulty, or that those who disagree with us are motivated by ill-will, ignorance or stupidity. The possibility that such disagreement may derive from the collision of different cultural norms is regarded with suspicion, given that no culture is easy with the relativization of its own moral norms.

In reality, everything that we do is culturally coded and our own universalist assumptions are never culturally innocent. There are, of course, structural similarities and parallels, and it is the task of the social sciences to identify them; but beyond a given threshold, difference prevails.[7] If we ignore these differences, we end up imposing our norms on others; the name for this is imperialism. Hence, in our understanding of modernity and democracy, we must recognize the pre-eminent role of cultural norms. This brings us to the problematic of culture itself.

All cultures are collective; they include and exclude; they give us a particular set of identities; they allow us to make sense of the world; they offer us collective regulation and collective forms of knowledge; and they are bounded. These boundaries may shift but they will not vanish. They protect the culture in question and act as a filter through which new ideas are received and integrated. All cultures rely on broadly similar mechanisms to keep themselves in being.[8] They engage in cultural reproduction and construct memory, a myth-symbol complex, forms of mutual recognition and the quest for acceptance of their moral worth as communities of value.[9] If threatened, they will redouble their efforts to protect cultural reproduction. Hence, in our analysis of cultures, it is vital to recognize that cultural reproduction has a rationality of its own, one that certainly defies material rationality and utilitarian satisfaction. Indeed, whenever you hear a particular pattern of collective behaviour by

---

7   Norbert Elias, *A szociológia lényege* [German title: *Was ist Soziologie*] (Budapest: Napvilág, 1998).
8   Fredrik Barth (ed.) *Ethnic Groups and Boundaries: The Social Organization of Culture Difference* (Bergen/Oslo: Universitetsforlaget, 1969); Hastings Donnan and Thomas M. Wilson, *Borders: Frontiers of Identity, Nation and State* (Oxford: Berg, 1999).
9   Elemér Hankiss, *Fears and Symbols* (Budapest-New York: CEU Press, 2000).

another group being described as "irrational", you can be certain that the speaker is making a statement about their own boundedness.

The problematic does not end there, however. If we can recognize the relationship between citizenship and culture, and the central significance of cultural reproduction, it follows that the rise of the modern state, with part of its base in the realm of culture, simultaneously means disproportion in power relations. Some states are evidently more powerful than others. This can be argued as a form of uneven development, though hardly in the Marxian sense. Put simply, the rise of a number of politically, economically, and militarily powerful states in Europe in the latter part of the eighteenth century threatened the cultural reproduction of other, less powerful communities. Once the early starters had been successful in condensing power around the political-cultural base, they threatened the cultural norms of other, less developed collectivities. The Napoleonic Wars were at least in part about this phenomenon. The weaker cultural communities had no option but respond or vanish, and few of them were prepared to face disappearance with equanimity. The patterns established then are still clearly recognisable.

The outcome was a frenzied race to construct modern – more accurately "modern" – cultures, cultural communities that could compete with the condensing power of the emergent modern states – France, Britain, the Netherlands, Denmark, Switzerland, Sweden. The difficulty for the latecomers was that they lacked the political, economic and cultural resources of the early entrants to modernity and were, therefore, obliged to construct a modernity from their own, inadequate resources. Without modernity and without autonomous access to political power, which did not necessarily have to mean state independence, they were doomed and they knew it. The literature of the latecomers in central and south eastern Europe, for instance, is full references to the fear of extinction.[10] This pattern then determines the history of Europe, as well as of nationhood, culture and democracy, until our time.

10　For examples see, Hans Kohn, *Nationalism: its Meaning and History* (Princeton: van Nostrand, 1955).

We are now in a position to see the quality of modern nationhood from a perspective that is different from the conventional view that privileges citizenship and universalism over culture and particularism, preferring to screen out the latter. Next, a few words on the relationship between culture and ethnicity. All cultures create identity, but not all identities are ethnic. Some identities are completely transient, others are restricted or contingent, yet others are partial. The particular qualities of ethnicity, however, demand further scrutiny. Ethnicity, and I am using the word in its European sense, not in its North American meaning of hyphenated identity, is to be understood as a culturally dense set of shared meanings that make the world coherent. A world of meanings is one of collective narratives that tell us what the world is about, what is positive and what is negative, why things happen and how we should behave. Without such meanings, the world is incoherent and terrifying. Individuals are left isolated and unable to cope. It follows that we all have both individual and collective identities. It is, again, naive to suppose otherwise.

Thus ethnicity is the web of meanings through which we understand and recognize one another and the world in which we live. It exists both in the explicit and the implicit dimension, in that ethnicity is part of the code through which we can take certain ideas, certain forms of knowledge for granted. When we say that something is "sensible" or that it is "common sense", we are tacitly referring to the ethnic forms of knowledge that we all have. There is nothing inherently reprehensible in this. The problems arise in the relationship between ethnicity and political power and that, as I have been arguing, is an inevitable and ineluctable aspect of modernity and thus of mass access to power through democracy. Nationhood, then, is constructed at the intersection of cultural reproduction and democratic political power.

The instruments of identity construction are complex, but may be unravelled by using some of the insights of sociology, anthropology, and cultural studies. My approach is post-Durkheimian. As far as I am concerned, collective identities are constructed and real for those living in them. A brief summary of these processes of identity construction yields something like this: collective and individual identities impact on one another reciprocally. There is a continuous construction of both the individual and the collective self, and some of this is implicit or occluded. Reflexive processes relativize our sense of identity, but do not eliminate them.[11]

A collective identity constructs a thought-world and a corresponding thought-style; these organize modes of thinking and the style of articulating them. Identities are anchored around a set of moral ideas, signifying that identity raises issues of "right" and "wrong", and that this is collective. The absence of moral regulation produces anomie, loss of identity and self.[12] The collective self is a collective identity. It creates collective forms of knowledge, it provides answers to a whole range of problems which exceed the capacity of the individual, like that of individual responsibility and remoteness of cause and effect. Collectivities are engaged in cultural reproduction and protection of the collective boundary. This is undertaken by reliance on a myth-symbol complex, boundary markers, and filters. Crucially, the collective identity creates and sustains a discursive field which holds meanings steady by establishing a plausibility structure.[13] Benedict Anderson's theory of imagining a collective existence functions implicitly by relying on the theory of discursive fields.[14] These discursive fields offer the individual stability and security and are the foundation for communication, as well as for providing a sense of identity over time. Crucially, the continuous definition and redefinition of identity requires an ongoing normative debate.[15] In the absence of such debate, norms are simply imposed on the weaker party.

And given the significance of discursive fields in sustaining collective existence, it is hardly surprising that all identity groups seek to minimize ambiguity and to establish as far as possible a single, unchallenge-

---

11   Mary Douglas, *How Institutions Think* (Syracuse NY: Syracuse University Press, 1986); Anthony Giddens, *The Consequences of Modernity* (Cambridge: Polity, 1990).

12   Emile Durkheim, *The Elementary Forms of Religious Life* (New York: Free Press, 1995).

13   Peter Berger, *The Sacred Canopy: Elements of a Sociological Theory of Religion* (New York: Doubleday, 1967).

14   Benedict Anderson, *Imagined Communities*, 2nd ed. (London: Verso, 1991).

15   Mary Douglas, *Risk and Blame: Essays in Cultural Theory* (London: Routledge, 1992).

able sense to utterances. Collectivities rely heavily on the production of monology – the elimination of ambiguity – whether of the thought-style or at the moment of receiving external ideas. It is equally clear that such monology is under perpetual challenge both from within and from outside. Monology cannot be sustained, but is a continuous endeavour of collective existence.[16]

Ultimately, collective identities give the individual's life a meaning beyond the individual lifetime, they are a way of constructing the past and the future. However, identities may be fractured by, for example, the impact of change (political, economic, technological) that bring the existing meanings into doubt. The outcome can be a devastating crisis for the collective in question.

From this brief sketch, it should be clear that identities and identity construction are a complex and often sensitive area, one that is frequently misunderstood, and the insensitivity of external actors with greater power than the community in question can have far-reaching negative consequences. The coming of modernity was a crisis of this kind for latecomers; and this process is continuous, given the dynamic, rapidly changing nature of the world today. National communities which think that they have adapted successfully to the demands of modernity discover that the goalposts have been shifted without their participation.

This now brings us to the next set of problems. We have become accustomed to journalists' sensationalist accounts of ethnicity, seen at this popular level as an unmitigated evil, and reinforced by our own inclination towards seeing our norms as universal, which leads us to undervalue or devalue the norms of others. We marginalize the role of solidarity in the construction of democracy overwhelmingly, because we in the West have been fortunate enough to live in solidly established democratic societies.

If we turn now to central and south eastern Europe, where new democracies are being constructed, it is far too easy to believe that these

---

16   Simon Dentith, *Bakhtinian Thought: an Introductory Reader* (London: Routledge, 1995); Michael Holquist, *Dialogism: Bakhtin and his World* (London: Routledge, 1990).

are unsuccessful or are solely operated for the benefit of ethnic majorities or sustain their thin democratic practices only because of the pressures of the West. A deeper analysis of nationhood produces a different conclusion. The central problem for the political communities emerging from communism a decade ago was the scarcity of materials from which to build democracy and, second, the problem – still a problem – of trying to build a democratic order that goes with the grain of cultural expectations.

The grain of cultural expectations is a metaphor, of course, and the central problem for the post-communist region was to establish a social base for a democratic order, one that goes beyond surface compliance. In central Europe, this has been broadly successful. There is both elite and popular acceptance of and support for democracy and there has been some movement towards the acceptance of the diversity and complexity that modernity produces, and towards giving some of this diversity a political representation. Of course, there are flaws and failures, and these are picked up and exaggerated by the Western press, but the overall trend is set to fair.

What the West – to be precise, the dominant states of the West – finds very difficult to understand and, therefore, to integrate into its perception of the region is the phenomenon of cultural insecurity. The mainstream history of Europe and the West has been written from the perspective of the successful actors and these have been the larger states. But there is another history, one written from the standpoint of the small state. This putative alternative viewpoint would give us a quite different picture. It would show, for example, that the dominant powers in Europe have consistently ignored the narratives of the smaller cultural communities and stigmatized them as provincial or irrational. If one looks at the past through eyes of the central or south eastern Europeans, the past is often malign and under the control of other, external forces.[17]

---

17 For a forceful argument of this in the case of south eastern Europe, see, Misha Glenny, *The Balkans 1804–1999: Nationalism, War and the Great Powers* (London: Granta, 1999).

This phenomenon, this sense of seeing oneself as marginal, on the periphery, has been an enduring aspect of the region.[18] But the smaller states of western Europe are not significantly different. Their central concern has been to match the capacity of the large states in condensing cultural and political power in order to develop their own domestic models of modernity. Scandinavia has been successful on the whole, as have the Low Countries and Portugal. But the experience of central and south eastern Europe points in the other direction.

Now this factor is relevant to the present day, because it helps to explain the role of ethnicity in the politics of the region. Given the pre-eminence of the larger states, the central and south eastern Europeans have repeatedly had to live with the experience of having externally developed models of modernity foisted upon them, often enough without a second thought as to their own norms and imperatives. Communism was the most extreme of these externally driven modernizations, but there have been many others in history, including modern history. Indeed, the reception of democracy and integration into the European Union has certain structural similarities with earlier transformations. Not unexpectedly, the sense of being at the mercy of external forces impels these communities, or at any rate some members of these communities, to retreat into their cultural citadels, into a cultural isolation, for fear that otherwise their cultural reproduction will be at risk. It is this fear for the continued existence of the community that underlies resonance of ethnic and ethnicized discourses. It is not the whole story, of course; the acceptance of democratic norms has been genuine, but the lack of time to construct their own responses and the impatience of the West have had their consequences.

In any case, small states and small cultural communities suffer certain disadvantages that large states seem quite incapable of understanding, or so the history of the last two centuries would suggest. On the one hand, access to power is clearly more direct in a small state – anything below a population of 20 million is small – because the number of levels

---

18   Czeslaw Milosz, *The Witness of Poetry* (Cambridge MA: Harvard University Press, 1983).

of representation is fewer. It is easier for individuals to make their mark. And the members of the elite come to know one another well. As against this, it is much more problematic to generate the kind of cultural density that large states can do, indeed do so without any conscious effort. As a result, small states are more exposed to external influences and need stronger barriers to protect their cultural norms. This necessarily leads them to adopt practices that are supportive of ethnicity and ethnic discourses, even when this flies in the face of the human rights normativity that large states have elaborated. It would help, if the larger states practised a measure of self-limitation, held back and tried understand the needs of smaller communities. But they do not do so. Nor do they engage them in normative debate, which is essential if the parties are to internalize values rather than merely react passively. Power implies responsibility, but political actors can find this responsibility difficult to discharge when it comes to other actors whom they do not recognize as fully equal.

An example from current events. It is clear to anyone who knows the dynamics of ethnic cultural reproduction that no amount of cajoling or bribery or threats will produce the kind of ethnic cooperation in Kosovo or Macedonia that the West is seeking to attain in the name of multi-culturalism. This is not because the Albanians, Serbs, and Macedonians are obstinate, recalcitrant or ill-intentioned, but because Western projects pay scant attention to their cultural fears. The best that can be attained at this time, in order to secure the minimum, is the institutionalization of parallel societies. But the West will not hear of this. The outcome is continued insecurity all round and no amount of Western money or pressure will change this. The local actors will pay lip-service to what they think the West wants to hear, but that is as far as they will go.

The proposition so far has been that the state acquired new power in the seventeenth and eighteenth centuries, that to exercise that power efficiently, it had to develop a reciprocal relationship between rulers and ruled and the redistribution of power was most effective within a relatively homogeneous culture. This indicates that from the outset, ethnicity – shared culture – was an integral part of democracy and that modern nationhood cannot be conceived of without the collective cultural norms condensed by the state. All this suggests that a high capacity state reliant on a web of shared cultural norms is a necessary condition for citizenship.

The problem at the start of the new millennium is that the established states of the West, which have constructed successful democracies, are coming under pressure from two disparate but related directions. From within, the explosion of civil society and the proliferation of civil social actors – lobbies, pressure groups, charities, semi-state agencies, identity movements, entitlement claimants – are transforming the nature of the relationship between rulers and ruled.[19] Not only is party politics weaker, but the authority of the central state bodies is declining. The state is losing its capacity to condense cultural power in the way that it could even in the very recent past. If it continues to lose this capacity, it could endanger civil society itself, as civil society without state regulation and enforcement of the rule of law rapidly becomes uncivil, as has happened in Russia.

Simultaneously, the power of the state is being eroded by globalization.[20] The consequences are likely to be an unexpected transformation of politics. Parallel to the growth of civil society, there could well be an increase in ethnic identification. States, finding that their capacity to condense civic power is under challenge, could come to rely more heavily on ethnic or ethnicized discourses. Large states are becoming smaller in the context of globalization. This does not have to be a disaster for democracy, as some fear. There are well-tried instruments for regulating inter-ethnic relations. What is beyond doubt is that the universalism of the great cultural powers, the belief that the French, British, or American way of doing things is best for everyone, will be challenged, and the diversity of cultures, articulated as ethnic identity, will find ever stronger expression.

19 Zygmunt Bauman, *In Search of Politics* (Cambridge: Polity, 1999).
20 John Urry, *Sociology beyond Societies: Mobilities for the Twenty-First Century* (London: Routledge, 2000); Zygmunt Bauman, *Globalization: The Human Consequences* (Cambridge: Polity, 1998).

www.ingramcontent.com/pod-product-compliance
Lightning Source LLC
Chambersburg PA
CBHW050237270326
41914CB00034BA/1954/J